Happy Birthday my
"Dear Fri..." ♡ **W9-AFV-569**

Love,
Debbie

A Miracle a Day

Also by Ann Spangler

An Angel a Day: Stories of Angelic Encounters

A Miracle a Day

Stories of Heavenly Encounters

ANN SPANGLER

ZondervanPublishingHouse

Grand Rapids, Michigan

A Division of HarperCollinsPublishers

A Miracle a Day
Copyright © 1996 by Ann Spangler

Requests for information should be addressed to:

📖 ZondervanPublishingHouse
Grand Rapids, Michigan 49530

ISBN: 0-310-20794-0

International Trade Paper Edition 0-310-21050-X

This edition printed on acid-free paper and meets the American National Standards Institute Z39.48 standard.

Interior design by Sherri L. Hoffman

Printed in the United States of America

98 99 00 01 02 03 /❖ DC/ 10 9 8 7 6 5

To Bob, Jim, and Mark
My three favorite brothers

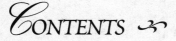ONTENTS ℬ

INTRODUCTION

*I*magine for a moment that one of your children is in danger. She is walking blindfolded toward the edge of a cliff. A few more steps and she will tumble to her death. You are standing a football field away. What do you do? Fortunately, you happen to have a megaphone in your hand. You shout through it, imploring her to stop and turn around before it's too late.

This is one way of understanding why God performs miracles. At times, they are his megaphone to children who have wandered into dangerous territory and to a world that has grown deaf to the divine voice. But miracles often happen to people who live close to God as well. Perhaps it is enough to say that miracles appear to be an extraordinary form of divine communication. They capture our attention in compelling ways.

Signs and wonders, the biblical terms for miracles, always convey some kind of spiritual message. And, as in any conversation, the message varies depending on the circumstances in which it is delivered. Sometimes a miracle reveals God's power, sometimes his mercy or his graciousness. Always, such wonders are a sign of the in-breaking of the divine kingdom, a down payment on our future with God.

I hope the stories that follow, both from Scripture and from ordinary men and women, will nourish your faith that God is still in control of our chaotic world. It is my conviction that the same God who met Moses in the desert and spoke to him from the midst of a fiery bush, longs to speak to us today—to tell us of his tender love, his power, and his desire to deliver us from harm. Whether you are standing at a cliff's edge or sitting before a cozy fire, I hope these stories will draw you closer to the only One who can be your refuge in every kind of trouble.

This book would not have been possible without the many men and women who were willing to tell their stories about how God has touched their lives. To them I am profoundly grateful. In fact, I received so many responses to my request for miracle stories, that I simply didn't have room enough to include them all in the pages of this book. To paraphrase Scripture, I am convinced that "of the making of miracles there is no end." Special thanks also go to *Our Sunday Visitor* and *New Covenant* magazine for kindly printing a letter of mine, soliciting stories from readers. Many others were also very gracious in helping me track down leads. In this regard, I am particularly grateful for the help of Nicky Cruz, Mary Ann Leland, Patti Matthews, Suzanne Morsfield, Pat Springle, Paul Thigpen, and Charles Turner. Lastly, I am thankful for the encouragement, critique, and friendship of two skilled editors: Sandy Vander Zicht and Bob Hudson, both of Zondervan. I am grateful for their insights and support.

In a few cases, names have been changed to protect the privacy of the individuals involved.

One

※

Miracles Happen When You Pray

Prayer enlarges the heart until it is capable of containing God's gift of Himself. Ask and seek and your heart will grow big enough to receive Him and keep Him as your own.
—MOTHER TERESA OF CALCUTTA

When faced with a dilemma or personal tragedy too large for any human being to handle, I have sometimes thrown up my hands and said: "All I can do is pray." Over the years, I have come to realize how ridiculous such a statement really is. It's as though I were to become frustrated with a piggy bank I couldn't open and said: "Well, all I can do is light this stick of dynamite and hope that it does something." That's what prayer is like—a spiritual explosive with the power to reconfigure the natural world.

That doesn't mean that every prayer we utter will result in a miracle. Despite our longings, a miracle may be the last thing that is needed. But it does mean that our requests are heard by the highest authority in the universe, by the only one both powerful and wise enough to answer our prayers effectively.

Like anything else, prayer takes practice. To learn to pray is to learn at least two basic lessons: surrender and persistence.

What exactly does it mean to surrender in prayer? Most often, we pray with definite ideas in mind. We think a problem will only be solved if God does this or that and does it right now. But the anxiety we bring to prayer can quickly transform our intercession into nothing more than an attempt to dictate to God. The first step, then, is to ask for grace to let go of our desire to control both the method and the outcome. As we do this, we will find our anxiety ebbing and a new peace taking hold as the Spirit reshapes our prayer according to God's will.

Besides surrender, we need to learn persistence. One of the greatest enemies of prayer is discouragement. We become disheartened because we pray and nothing seems to happen. Worse yet, the situation we are praying for deteriorates. Jesus himself spoke of the necessity of persistence when he encouraged his followers to keep asking God for what they needed. Persistence is, in fact, the yeast of prayer.

You may be thinking right now of an urgent prayer. Take time to quiet yourself in the presence of God. Ask him to deal with your anxiety and show you how to pray so that you might take your place next to Jesus, who is always interceding at the right hand of the Father.

The Wedding Miracle

~❦~

When the wine was gone, Jesus' mother said to him. "They have no more wine." "Dear woman, why do you involve me?" Jesus replied, "My time has not yet come." His mother said to the servants, "Do whatever he tells you." (JOHN 2:3–5)

*I*f anyone ever had perfect timing it was Jesus. He never missed a beat. In tune with his Father's will, he would only embark on his public ministry when God gave the go ahead, not before. So why does he seem to change his mind so quickly? Why does he perform a miracle that started tongues wagging all over Galilee?

Somehow he must have known that Mary's prayer had changed things, suddenly setting his public ministry in motion. Jesus' hidden life had come to an end. Now the light of the world would reveal itself, a counterpoint against the darkness.

Jesus wastes no time, ordering the servants to take six stone water jars, the kind the Jews used for ceremonial cleansing, and fill them with water. Then he tells them to call the steward so that he can draw out the water and taste it. As soon as it passes his lips, the man recognizes it as the most exquisite wine he has ever tasted, and he cannot imagine why the bride and groom have withheld the best wine until last.

As usual, the miracle is about more than a simple wedding feast in Cana. It is about transforming the ordinary into the extraordinary, the natural into the supernatural, the kingdom of this world into the kingdom of God, law into grace, and death into life. It is about the blood of a Savior whose body would be broken on a tree, so that from it would flow streams of living water. It is about a wedding feast in heaven to be celebrated at the end of time. It is about mercy, joy, and communion. And about the passionate love of God for his people.

Remarkably, this wonderful miracle came about because Mary noticed someone else's need and brought it to her son's attention. Because of the simple prayer of a compassionate woman, grace was released that set the saving plan of God in motion. It may even be that the Father was waiting for a prayer like hers before shifting things into high gear. Whatever the case, we should be encouraged. This miracle urges us to pray. For we are not merely members of the audience, passively entertained by the drama of salvation. Our prayers actually help to set the stage and may even raise the curtain on the next act of God's work in the history of the world.

Lord, it amazes me that your power accomplishes so many things at once. With this miracle, you encouraged us to pray, you showed compassion to a poor family, you began your reign, and you gave your people a glimpse of your plan of salvation. I am always astonished by the wonderful efficiency or your grace. Help me to recognize the needs of others and then to calmly and confidently call them to your attention. Like Mary, let me trust you to answer my prayer as you see fit.

Lost and Found

Again, I tell you that if two of you on earth agree about anything you ask for, it will be done for you by my Father in heaven. For where two or three come together in my name, there am I with them. (MATTHEW 18:19–20)

Alan Smith and his wife, Leisa, had spent part of the day raking leaves and pine straw from his mother-in-law's backyard. His young daughter, Lydia, was helping grandma too, in typical four-year-old fashion. They worked hard through the afternoon and as twilight edged across the horizon, they straightened their backs, stretched, and looked with satisfaction on their handiwork.

The yard looked great. The huge pine trees shimmered green against the deepening blue sky. Beautiful as they were, these trees had made a mess of the yard, yielding twelve bags full of pine straw. Now the black lawn bags were piled together in the middle of the grass.

Their sense of satisfaction was cut short as Leisa suddenly exclaimed, "Oh, no! My ring is gone. It could be anywhere on the lawn or in one of those bags." Her diamond engagement ring had slipped off her finger as she worked.

"We all felt sick, but I decided we could do something about it," explained Alan. "So I said, 'Let's just pray right now. God knows where it is.' We sat down on the grass and asked him to show one of us where the ring was. We closed our eyes and just stayed quiet for a minute.

Suddenly, my four-year-old jumped up and said, 'I know where it is!' She walked over to all those bags of pine straw and pulled one out. It wasn't the first one or the one on the edge either. Lydia went to one in the middle of all the bags and said, 'Open this one.' We didn't even have to dump the contents out. As soon as I opened it and spilled a little of the straw, out came the ring!"

What a wonderful experience for this small family! To pray together for their need and to see God use the tiniest member to perform a miracle. That day, the Smith family rejoiced, not just because something of value was restored to them but because something very precious was added to their faith.

Lord, you tell us that only those who become like little children will enter your kingdom. Give me the simple humility and faith of a child as I seek you for the desires closest to my heart. Then help me to follow your leading as you answer my prayers.

The Prayer of a Child

Which of you, if his son asks for bread, will give him a stone? Or if he asks for a fish, will give him a snake? If you, then, though you are evil, know how to give good gifts to your children, how much more will your Father in heaven give good gifts to those who ask him! (MATTHEW 7:9–11)

Most small children would choose a candy bar over an apple any day. But Andrew Weigand wasn't just any three-and-a-half-year-old. He had never tasted the tartness of an apple or savored the sound of one snapping crisply between his teeth. For that matter, he never ate pears, oranges, plums, grapes, cherries, strawberries, blueberries, raspberries, watermelon, peaches, apricots, nectarines, or any other kind of fruit under the sun except bananas. Since infancy, he suffered from severe food allergies that would cause him to pay for the slightest mistake with a blistery rash and a bad case of diarrhea. As a baby, he would scream every time he wet his diaper.

To make matters worse, Andrew attended a toddler's group in church that was forever singing a cheery little song that went like this: "Who can make an apple? I'm sure I can't. Can you? Oh, who can make an apple? Only God can. It is true." Then each of the kids would be given a piece of fake fruit and the adults would talk about how fruit is good for you, how God wants kids to have the fruit of the Spirit, and how God gives fruit to make us healthy. More than anything, Andrew wanted to be able to eat an apple like the other kids. His mother, Marie, could see the conflict playing out in his young mind. "We can pray, Andrew," she told him. "That's all we can do. Mommy doesn't have a medicine that will take care of the problem, but Jesus might heal you if we ask him."

It's little wonder that Marie got so frustrated that one day she actually brought some plastic vegetables to the group and asked the adults to start singing about carrots, cucumbers, and potatoes. They did so good-naturedly, but Andrew still wanted to be like the other kids.

A couple of months later she decided to take her son to a healing service at a local church. At one point the man who was leading the prayer service said he believed God was healing someone of severe food allergies. "My heart jumped," said Marie. "I placed my hand on Andrew's head and asked God to deal with the allergies. But I still wasn't sure anything had happened, so I decided to take him up front for more prayer. During the entire service, I experienced a tremendous sense of peace, but I really didn't know whether my son had been healed.

"All the way home a friend who was with us kept repeating, 'Andrew, you're healed! You're going to go home and eat an apple.' Her certainty irritated me, and I kept hushing her because I didn't want to get Andrew's hopes up. But it was too late.

"When I suggested he start with a small slice of apple, he looked at me and said, 'You know I'm healed. I don't know why you're not giving me the whole thing.' I was reluctant to trust the faith of a toddler, but my husband encouraged me to give it a try so I did. I braced myself for the inevitable, but nothing happened, not the slightest rash, no diarrhea, nothing. A few months earlier, a one-inch cube of watermelon was enough to set off a violent reaction. But that day Andrew ate the apple like any other healthy kid. Now he eats grapes like crazy and spreads cherry jam on his bagel. He has had absolutely no problems with any kind of food allergy.

"I really don't know why God healed Andrew when so many people suffer from much more serious problems, but I do know that this is one mother and son who never doubt that our God is a God of love and mercy."

Father, you know how hard it is for us to see our children suffer. We feel so helpless and frustrated by their pain. When this happens, help us to remember that we are utterly dependent on you just as our children are dependent on us. May we come to you with a child's confidence that you are who you say you are—a loving and all-powerful Father, one who pays attention to our prayers and answers them with both wisdom and mercy.

A Miracle of Sheer Persistence

"That you may know that the Son of Man has authority on earth to forgive sins…" He said to the paralytic, "I tell you, get up, take your mat and go home." He got up, took his mat and walked out in full view of them all. (MARK 2:10–12)

A crowd had gathered to hear Jesus speak in Capernaum, on the edge of the shores of Galilee. People were jammed into the house where he was preaching, anxious to catch sight of the man who had cast out demons and even cured a leper. Many Pharisees were there as well. Believers and skeptics filled the room. People spilled out the doorway, like too many beans in a jar. Everyone wanted to hear what the rabbi was saying inside.

Four men approached, carrying a man who was paralyzed. They too had heard the wonderful stories about Jesus. Perhaps he would do something for their friend whose twisted limbs lay like so many branches strewn carelessly across the mat on which he lay. But so thick was the crowd that they couldn't push through. Undeterred, the men lifted their friend to the roof and began to remove the tile and thatch that covered it. As they worked, they could hear the voice of Jesus below.

At first the crowd seemed oblivious to what was happening. Suddenly, Jesus stopped speaking, every voice was hushed, and all eyes were fixed on the paralytic as he made his slow descent from the ceiling.

Delighted by the faith of the men who had lowered him through the roof, Jesus said to the paralytic: "Son, your sins are forgiven."

His words astonished the Pharisees. They knew the law and the law said that God alone could forgive sins.

"This man is a fraud. He is blaspheming God!" Instantly, Jesus discerned their unspoken thoughts and said to them, "Why are you thinking these things? Which is easier: to say to the paralytic, 'Your sins are forgiven,' or to say, 'Get up, take your mat and walk'? But that you may know that the Son of Man has authority on earth to forgive sins . . ." He said to the paralytic, "I tell you, get up, take your mat and go home." He got up, took his mat, and walked out in full view of them all. This amazed everyone and they praised God, saying, "We have never seen anything like this!"

Anyone could have spoken a word of false comfort to the paralyzed man, telling him his sins were forgiven, but only God had the power to enable him to get off his mat and walk out the door. Clearly, this Jesus had power over the soul as well as the body. The Pharisees had needed a tangible sign that Jesus could forgive sins. Perhaps the paralytic himself had needed proof that his sins were forgiven. How could he doubt it now? His arms and legs were straight, his mat was in his hand, and he was striding away from the house a new man.

The people had seen the invalid's atrophied limbs. But Jesus had seen his atrophied soul. So he dealt with what was inside the man before touching and restoring what was on the outside.

So often, we come to God asking for a miracle: to cure a sick friend, bring back a wayward child, heal an eating disorder, save a troubled marriage. We think we know what will make us whole and happy again. But God always penetrates the surface of our need to deal with the core problem. He is not interested in performing miracles that only display his power. He wants to perform miracles that reveal his love. And so he deals, not just with our pain, but with the source of our pain, not just with the infirmity of our bodies, but with the infirmity of our hearts. Like the paralytic's friends, we *are* called to pray with faith. As we do, God will forgive our sins and then touch us with his power.

Father, sometimes it is easier for me to believe in your power than in your mercy. Help me to be quick to surrender my sins to your mercy, rather than stubbornly standing in judgment of myself. Give me assurance, as you did the man paralyzed by sin, that you really have forgiven me. Finally, grant me the same persistent love and bold faith of the men who lowered their brother, the paralytic, into the presence of Jesus. Then let me trust him for the results.

The Miracle of Persistent Love

I have heard your prayer and seen your tears; I will heal you.
(2 KINGS 20:5)

ob Mardock was associate pastor at the Eugene Friends Church in Eugene, Oregon, when it happened. He and other members of the church conducted a prayer service every Tuesday. Anyone who wanted, could come for extended times of prayer, often lasting for two or three hours for one person. They called it soaking prayer.

"One day, a woman I'll call Jean came in for prayer. She was a tough case. Diagnosed with lupus, she had been given six months to live. Her hair was falling out, her face was bloated, her skin was scaly, and she looked really awful. But we said we would pray and so we did. Actually, we prayed for her every week for six months. During that time, she began to tell us many things about her past that we were able to pray through. As a young woman she had been the victim of incest and had suffered all kinds of physical and emotional abuse. Hooked on drugs, she had eventually gotten pregnant. Her life was a mess, but we kept praying. Gradually, she got better. Her skin cleared up, her hair started to grow back, and she felt great. This woman was verging on death when we first met her. After six months of prayer, we saw her life transformed like a living miracle. Not only was her body healthy but her soul was restored. Years of sin and abuse had been surrendered to God and healed.

"I stayed in touch with Jean for a few years. As it turned out, she was especially gifted in praying for others. At one point, she was hired to head up the prayer ministry at a church in Washington. I can't offer you proof positive that the lupus never returned, though I have no reason to think it did. Whatever the case, I am absolutely certain that God performed a miracle in her life through prayer."

Jean's story reminds us that God wants to heal our souls as well as our bodies. How easy it would be for him to simply wave his almighty hand and command our symptoms to disappear. For many of us, that's all we really want. We'd rather not dig too deeply to expose the root of our problems. But fortunately, God is never content to merely treat our symptoms. Instead, he prescribes a remedy that is often administered through the loving hands and hearts of ordinary people, friends who will not let us go no matter how hard and long the road to healing may be.

Father, it's your love that heals us, body and soul. Thank you for the way you reveal this tremendous love through other people. Help me to realize that persistent prayer is nothing other than persistent love. May I remember this when I am tempted to quit praying. As I persist, reveal your love through me.

Two

Miracles of Healing

I believe in miraculous cures, and I shall never forget the impact I felt watching with my own eyes how an enormous cancerous growth on the hand of a worker dissolved and changed into a light scar. I cannot understand, but I can even less doubt what I saw with my own eyes.

—DR. ALEXIS CARREL, NOBEL PRIZE IN MEDICINE, 1913

*I*t was no surprise that my request for miracle stories generated more descriptions of physical healing than any other kind of miracle. As creatures in a fallen world, we often feel our separation from paradise most acutely in our bodies. Illness, in fact, is often a precursor of death and is, itself, a smaller kind of death. Interestingly, Paul's Letter to the Romans traces the root of our problem: it tells us that the wages of sin is death.

As Louis Mondon, the author of *Signs and Wonders*, has pointed out, the flesh is the "theatre of the redemptive work." So it makes sense that God would sometimes heal our bodies as a way of revealing his mercy and saving grace.

In fact, when God touches our flesh it is to impart a deeper message to our spirits. Ultimately, this is what gives lasting significance to such miracles. Otherwise, every miracle of healing performed on mortal creatures would eventually be undone.

As Monden points out, miracles of healing have more in common with Christ's transfiguration on Mount Tabor than with his Resurrection. On Tabor the veil was lifted for a moment, to reveal Jesus' glory to his disciples. But the decisive victory had not yet been won. Jesus still had to face Gethsemane and Golgotha. So too we still face suffering and sorrow and many trials in the years that are left to us. To echo the familiar words of the poet Robert Frost, we yet have many "miles to go before we sleep."

If you or someone you love is suffering from some kind of physical or mental disorder, I hope you will take heart from the stories that follow. Who knows whether God will stretch out his hand and touch you with a miracle? But whether he does or not, never stop clinging to him. For one day he will wipe every tear from your eyes, and "there will be no more death or mourning or crying or pain." For the old order of things will have finally passed away.

An Enemy Healed

*When Jesus' followers saw what was going to happen, they said,
"Lord, should we strike with our swords?" And one of them struck the
servant of the high priest, cutting off his right ear. But Jesus answered,
"No more of this!" And he touched the man's ear and healed him.*
(LUKE 22:49–51)

A few years ago, I had the opportunity of visiting Israel with
a small group of friends. One day we were traveling
through a region northeast of Tel Aviv when we passed through the
valley of Armageddon, the place where the Book of Revelation pin-
points the world's last battle. As our small bus traveled past this fore-
boding place, I noticed one of my fellow passengers asleep across the
aisle. Later, we joked that Bill was the only person we knew who had
actually slept through Armageddon.

Centuries earlier, Jesus' disciples managed to sleep through one
of the darkest moments in salvation history. After the Passover Meal
they followed him to the Mount of Olives. As Jesus agonized in prayer
about his coming suffering, his followers dozed off. But as soon as they
awoke, they found themselves faced with a detachment of soldiers and
officials from the chief priests and Pharisees, intent on arresting their
master.

Taken by surprise, they asked Jesus whether they should draw
their swords against the crowd. Without waiting for his reply, Peter cut

off the ear of Malchus, servant to the high priest. But Jesus rebuked Peter, picked up the man's ear, and proceeded to fasten it in place as though it had never been torn from his head.

I wonder who was more surprised: Malchus or Peter? Why would a man with this kind of power use it to heal his enemy? Why would he allow himself to be arrested in the first place? It was too much for Peter and the disciples, who promptly abandoned Jesus to his fate.

With the benefit of hindsight, we recognize how foolish Peter was. But as usual, this impetuous follower of Christ acts as a mirror reflecting our own behavior. How do we respond when the gospel comes under attack—in the media, in our schools, in our neighborhoods, or in the political arena? What happens when we come under some kind of personal attack? Do we fortify ourselves with prayer, asking for grace to know and be faithful to the divine strategy as Jesus did in Gethsemane? Or have we too fallen asleep in the hour of darkness? Once we awaken to the threat, do we respond like Peter, thinking that Jesus is too weak to defend himself? If so, we may resort to dirty tricks and name calling, demonizing anyone who opposes us. In our fear, we may circle the wagons and reduce the gospel of Christ to mere politics.

But the lesson of Gethsemane is that we must join Jesus as he prays to the Father for the strength to do his will. Only then will we be given the necessary grace to respond in faith rather than fear, in courage rather than self-defensiveness.

Lord, I thank you that Peter was far from perfect. His mistakes somehow manage to encourage me. Even though he was one of your closest friends and followers, he often misunderstood you and entirely missed the point. But still you were patient with him, and his faith grew strong in the process. Help me to learn from my mistakes, and teach me how to pray in your presence.

Healing Presence

Therefore my heart is glad and my tongue rejoices; my body also will rest secure, because you will not abandon me to the grave, nor will you let your Holy One see decay. You have made known to me the path of life; you will fill me with joy in your presence, with eternal pleasures at your right hand. (PSALM 16:9–11)

With several best-selling books to her credit, Catherine Marshall was a woman many of us will not soon forget. In her book *Meeting God at Every Turn* she tells a remarkable story about her struggle with tuberculosis. Diagnosed in 1943 at Johns Hopkins in Baltimore, she was devastated to hear the news that she would need three to four months of complete bed rest. She could only get up to use the bathroom. How could she possibly confine her world to a sickbed when her three-year-old son needed her, she worried. Little did she know those few months would stretch into two frustrating years as each visit to the doctor revealed absolutely no improvement.

Fortunately, her enforced rest was anything but wasted. Catherine spent her time reading Scripture and exploring God's character, asking him the hard questions of faith and probing beneath the surface for the answers she sought. Not surprisingly, one of her questions had to do with whether God still healed people. As a child she had learned that miracles had ceased with the early church. Yet page after page of the gospels revealed a Jesus who loved to heal people. So eager was he to touch the sick, blind, and lame with his healing power that he couldn't wait even twenty-four hours to avoid performing a miracle on the Sabbath—a practice that deeply offended the religious authorities of his day. How could this same Jesus refrain from healing people for two thousand years? She didn't believe he could or would. So she and her husband, Peter, prayed fervently for a miracle. But none came.

Still, they continued to pray. Finally, after many days of internal struggle, Catherine uttered an honest prayer of complete abandonment, telling God he could do whatever he wanted with her. She would accept his will even if it meant she would be an invalid for the rest of her life. He didn't have to explain himself to her, because she trusted him to love and provide for her no matter what happened. That prayer was a turning point. The same night, while staying with her parents, she had an experience that changed her life:

"In the middle of that night I was awakened. The room was in total darkness. Instantly sensing something alive, electric in the room, I sat bolt upright in bed. Past all credible belief, suddenly, unaccountably, Christ was there, in Person, standing by the right side of my bed. I could see nothing but a deep, velvety blackness around me, but the bedroom was filled with an intensity of power, as if the Dynamo of the universe were there. Every nerve in my body tingled with it, as with a shock of electricity. I knew that Jesus was smiling at me tenderly, lovingly, whimsically—as though a trifle amused at my too-intense seriousness about myself. His attitude seemed to say, 'Relax! There's not a thing wrong here that I can't take care of.'"

Then she heard a voice instruct her to "go and tell her mother." This puzzled and frightened her. It was after all, the middle of the night. What was she supposed to say to her mother? Would her mother think she had lost her senses?

Still, she had the feeling that her future depended on her obedience. "I groped my way into the dark hall to the bedroom directly across from mine and spoke softly to Mother and Dad. Startled, Mother sat bolt upright in bed. 'Catherine, is anything wrong? What— what on earth has happened?'

"'It's all right,' I reassured them. 'I just want to tell you that I'll be all right now. It seemed important to tell you tonight. I'll give you the details tomorrow.'"

Soon after, X-rays showed a marked improvement in Catherine's condition. The long siege was drawing to a close. Within six months, the doctors pronounced her completely well.

So often it seems we can only learn the lessons of faith the hard way—by wrestling with God in the midst of whatever darkness he allows in our lives. But if we wrestle as Catherine Marshall did, with a determination to know God better, we will one day enjoy a deeper sense of his presence. We may even sense that he's smiling at us, telling us to relax in the knowledge that there's not a thing wrong that he can't take care of.

Lord, I'm a fighter by nature. "Never give up" is my life motto. If one thing won't work, then I'll try another and another and another. Help me to realize when it's time to fight and when it's time to surrender. You know the areas in my life that require surrender. Right now, I ask for the help to relinquish these to you. Give me the grace to say yes to your will. Not a yes spoken through gritted teeth, but an honest yes, spoken in a quiet place in my soul, the place where you dwell.

A Miracle of the Mind

*Then Jesus said to his disciples, "If anyone would come after me, he must deny himself and take up his cross and follow me. For whoever wants to save his life will lose it, but whoever loses his life for me will find it. (*MATTHEW 16:24–25)

Philip Luebbert had a lot going for him. Raised in a loving family, he excelled in school, and even made the dean's list in college. A serious young man, his faith meant a lot to him, and he enrolled in a seminary in St. Paul, Minnesota, to fulfill his childhood dream of becoming a priest. But by the time Philip was twenty-one, his dream was shattered. Though he didn't know it then, his mind was being overtaken by a terrible disease. Philip was suffering from schizophrenia.

"Unless you have lived through it, you cannot possibly imagine the horror that fills your mind—the terror that distorts your view of the world. You have emotions that most people will never experience," Philip explains. "I would be in a baseball stadium, for instance, and would be convinced that everybody was staring at me. Thousands of eyes just looking at Phil Luebbert. I became obsessed with religion, convinced that God was punishing me. And no matter what anyone said to me, I refused to get help.

"It got so bad that one day, when I was twenty-three, I simply lost it. I got into my car and started driving. I drove as fast as I could, straight for a bridge embankment. But suddenly, and I really don't know how this happened, I felt compelled to put my foot on the brake. It was as though some kind of irresistible force inside me made me switch my foot from the gas to the brakes. I crashed into the embankment but at a much slower speed. The car was totaled, but I walked away from the wreck—and straight into a mental hospital. From there it seemed like an endless stream of hospitals and doctors, and all of them said the same thing. Philip Luebbert would never hold down a job. He would never be able to live on his own. He would never have much of a life.

"I couldn't stop asking God, 'Why me? What did I ever do to deserve this? All I ever wanted was to live for you and serve you.' I felt so betrayed. But despite my questions, I couldn't rid myself of the notion that God was, after all, a loving God who was powerful enough to heal me. Deep down, I knew he wouldn't abandon me, and I continued to pray regularly and ask his forgiveness whenever I felt I offended him. The church was a haven for me throughout this time. Despite my confusion, I just couldn't give up on God—and he didn't give up on me.

"My healing didn't happen overnight. But gradually I began to improve, and in 1987 I landed my first job—as a dishwasher. It wasn't the job I dreamed of as a young man, but after what I had been through, it was astonishing that I could work at all. I thought my folks would explode with joy when I told them the news. My life will never be what I thought it would be as a young boy. I know the ravages of the disease still linger to some degree. But anyone who knew me during the years of my hospitalization would tell you that a tremendous miracle of healing has occurred in my life.

"I still don't know why I have had to struggle with this disease. But through it I have come to love the cross of Christ. I now know without a doubt that suffering can be redemptive. When I didn't know what to do, when there was no place to go for help, when I was on the verge of despair, I just kept clinging to God. And he was there. He saved me. He restored me. And he has a purpose for my life."

Father, each of us has a cross to bear in this life—some sorrow or suffering that shapes our souls for better or worse. Whatever it may be, help us to take courage from the cross of your Son. May we hold fast to you no matter what. And as we cling to you, mold us with your loving hands and shape us into your likeness.

A Remedy for Tooth Decay

Where is the wise man? Where is the scholar? Where is the philosopher of this age? Has not God made foolish the wisdom of the world?
(1 CORINTHIANS 1:20)

I don't know about you, but somehow it's easier for me to believe that Jesus can heal a severed ear, a malignant tumor, or sightless eyes than it is to believe that he can even perform a dental miracle if he wants to, but that's what happened to Rose Marie Cruz.

Rose Marie and Bobby Cruz were attending a prayer service in someone's home when it happened. Both of them were new believers, and unbeknown to Rose Marie, Bobby had been praying for a miracle to reassure him that God was real.

A guest speaker had been invited to pray with people that night, and Rose Marie was determined to ask for healing. She had been smoking for seventeen years, and it showed. Three packs a day had wreaked havoc in her mouth. Her teeth were so badly discolored that she hated to smile. Despite Bobby's cautions, she went forward for prayer. As she did, she had a remarkable experience. Suddenly, she explained, she found herself on the floor, oblivious to what was happening around her. When Bobby saw his wife keel over, he rushed to the front of the room, yelling at the man who had prayed with her, "You've killed my wife, you've killed my wife!" But something strange was happening to Rose Marie.

Someone yelled, "Look at her mouth!" A white foam-like substance covered her lips. When Rose Marie regained her senses, she described her experience like this: "My mouth felt like it does after you visit the dentist and they put that gel in to clean your teeth. Later I looked in the mirror and my teeth were perfectly white. Also, several of my teeth were filled. I distinctly remember a friend of mine who saw the whole thing saying, 'I see it, but I don't believe it.' I wouldn't have believed it either if it hadn't happened to me. Afterward I went to my dentist, who asked me: 'What is this you have in your teeth? What kind of chemical is it? What is it made of?' When I told him the story, he said, 'No, no, no, I don't want to hear it.' I guess they don't prepare you for that kind of thing in dental school.

"Later, I was examined by six dentists, all of whom corroborated the fact that my teeth were sound. It was such a great sign to both Bobby and me that God was real and that he cared about us. Shortly after it happened, Bobby used to wake up in the middle of the night, look in my mouth and say, 'It's still there. You know, God really loves us.'

"Still, it took me three more months to stop smoking. I felt bad about it but didn't know what to do. Finally I told God, 'If I'm your temple, I cannot continue to hurt myself by smoking. Please help me to quit.' After that, I just stopped. Bobby would bring home cartons of cigarettes for a while, but I would just throw them away. He couldn't understand why I would waste money like that. He didn't really believe I had quit. But I had. It's been twenty-three years and I have never touched another cigarette.

"Having your mouth healed is a wonderful miracle. But having your life changed is even more of a miracle. People tend to turn to God when they have a problem. I figure if God could do so many great things in our lives, there's nothing he can't handle."

Father, sometimes I feel a little embarrassed by the things you do and the way you do them. Then I remember that "the foolishness of God is wiser than man's wisdom, and the weakness of God is stronger than man's strength." Help me to grow in the kind of wisdom that welcomes your work wherever I encounter it.

One Miracle at a Time

He lifted me out of the slimy pit, out of the mud and mire; he set my feet on a rock and gave me a firm place to stand. He put a new song in my mouth, a hymn of praise to our God. (PSALM 40:2–3)

Carlene Miller's livelihood depended on her voice. She was on the phone constantly negotiating lease agreements with other companies. In 1993 she came down with what she thought was a bad case of laryngitis. But it was worse than that. A specialist told her she was suffering from a paralyzed vocal chord, probably as a result of a virus. Time would tell whether it would heal or whether her voice would be reduced to a whisper for the rest of her life. There was nothing the specialist could do.

The thought was intolerable to Carlene, who also enjoyed a singing ministry in local churches. Now she could neither sing nor talk in a normal voice. After three or four words, she would have to pause for breath. At work, she wrote scripts for her secretary, hoping to get by until her voice returned. But it just wasn't working.

Still, the specialist told her that her chances of recovery were good, though it would take up to six months. It had already been five weeks, and Carlene wondered if she could stand another day of it. To make matters worse, she had recently been diagnosed with chronic fatigue syndrome. She worried that she might lose her job.

"I was so crushed by the news," she said, "that I went home and cried on my roommate, Sally's, shoulder. Later, I got a call from someone at church inviting me to attend the weekly worship team practice the next evening. Even though I couldn't sing a note, I agreed to go because my friends there wanted to pray for me.

"But I had to work late the next day and was exhausted as a result of my chronic fatigue. All I could think of was how much I wanted to lie down. If I could just get some sleep. But Sally, who wasn't particularly religious, insisted I go to church. 'Normally, I would tell you to stay home,' she said, 'but the people in your church want to pray for you, and I think you should go. I'll even drive you.'

"So we went and Sally sat in the back watching as the choir surrounded me to pray for my healing. They prayed out loud and then began singing. After about twenty minutes of this, some of the members began playing instruments. It turned into an impromptu worship fest, and the music was so beautiful that I almost forgot why I was there. The presence of God was so palpable I began to cry.

"Suddenly I had this strange notion that I should open my mouth and shout at the top of my lungs. It seemed ridiculous. How could I shout when talking was so impossible? I had hardly been able to whisper for five weeks. But the thought kept getting stronger until I couldn't stand it anymore. So I just yelled, 'It's back!' and then everyone started to cry. Somehow God gave me the faith to shout that my voice was healed before I even knew it.

"On the way home, Sally kept saying,: 'If I hadn't driven you here and heard you try to talk for the past several weeks, I wouldn't have believed it.'

"After that, my voice was strong as ever, except that I lost some range in my singing, which returned after a few months' practice. I was so overjoyed and full of faith that I just knew I would wake up the next morning without even a symptom of my chronic fatigue. The God I worshiped was a God of miracles. But I awoke feeling as tired as ever. The chronic fatigue was there in full force. I wondered why God would heal my voice but not the rest of me. It would be a while before I began to comprehend his reasons. But now I knew without a doubt that God cared about what was happening to me and that he was in control of my life."

Lord, you are a God who hears even our inaudible cries, a loving King who inhabits the praises of his people. As we come into your healing presence, let the music of our voices blend to form a refrain of praise that you will find beautiful to listen to.

Three

❧

Miracles that Multiply

Miracles do not happen in contradiction of nature, but in contradiction of what we know about nature.
—SAINT AUGUSTINE

*E*ven in an affluent society, so many of our problems seem to stem from scarcity. We feel we have too little money, too little time, too little love and patience. No matter how much money we set aside, we still worry about the future. Will inflation erode our nest egg? Will college costs keep soaring? How will we possibly find the time and energy to care for aging parents? Somehow, there is not enough of us, or the things we need, to go around. We are finite creatures with infinite aspirations.

When I am feeling this way, I like to recall the miracles of multiplication that God has already performed. As always, there is more to these miracles than meets the eye. When Jesus breaks the bread and it is multiplied, he offers us a glimpse of himself as the Bread of Life. When the disciples enjoy a record catch of fish, we realize they are to become fishers of men's souls. Scratch the surface of a miracle and you will find layers of spiritual meaning. Reduce the miraculous merely to its literal meaning and you will miss the point entirely.

So the next time you feel spiritually hungry, remind Jesus that he is, after all, the Bread of Life. The next time you run up against your limitations, use them as an opportunity to become more dependent on him. Be honest about your spiritual emptiness. Wrestle with Jesus' words, his promises, and his wonders until your soul finds the nourishment it craves. Give God what little you have—of faith, of desire, of perseverance—and ask him to multiply it a hundredfold.

An Education in Miracles

Taking the five loaves and the two fish and looking up to heaven, he [Jesus] gave thanks and broke the loaves. Then he gave them to the disciples and the disciples gave them to the people. They all ate and were satisfied, and the disciples picked up twelve basketfuls of broken pieces that were left over. (MATTHEW 14:19–20)

*Y*ou remember the story. Jesus and his disciples had just heard the news of John the Baptist's beheading. Now they sought a quiet place to make sense of this new sorrow. But the clamoring crowd followed and met them on the shore as they crossed the Sea of Galilee. As the boat drew near, Jesus could see them and hear their exultant shouts: "I see him!" "There he is, the miracle-worker!" "The one that drives out devils and even raises the dead!" There were so many of them: the sick in soul, the lepers, the sightless ones, the lame, the prostitutes and beggars. Each one had a hope, each a need. He knew their stories without asking.

He had been longing for rest, but his heart was stirred with compassion for the men and women thronging the shore. He spent the day moving among them, teaching them and healing the sick. But as evening approached, his disciples began to worry. What would happen when the sun went down? They were in a remote place with nothing to feed the crowd, which by now had swollen to several thousand people. Eight months' wages wouldn't be enough to feed a group this large.

47

So they did what you and I probably would have done. They suggested the obvious: Jesus should disperse the crowd so that each man could find food for his family in the surrounding villages. But Jesus astonished them with his reply: "How many loaves do you have?" They must have wondered why he would even ask such a crazy question. It would be like asking how many hot-dogs you had in your sack lunch to feed the fans in Yankee Stadium. "Five *small* loaves and two *small* fish," was their answer, as if to emphasize how little they had to meet such an enormous need.

Then Jesus asked the disciples to get the people to sit down in groups on the grass, and he proceeded to give thanks for the loaves, break them, and distribute them, along with the fish, to feed more than five thousand men, women, and children.

I love this picture of Jesus. Taking the small loaves and raising them to heaven and thanking his Father. It was as though he were saying, "Whatever you give, Father, is enough to do the job." And it was. The disciples kept handing out the bread and the fish, and the people kept eating. At the end of the day, everyone was full and twelve baskets of food were left over—one for each disciple.

Jesus and his disciples had been tired, sick at heart, longing for some peace and quiet. The last thing they desired was to spend the day with an endless stream of people, each one expecting a miracle. But once again the love and compassion of Jesus prevailed. What an experience his disciples must have had as their concern gave way to confusion, and confusion to wonder, and wonder to joy. Five small loaves had fed a multitude and they themselves had been instruments of the miracle, laughing as they dipped their hands into the baskets, scooping out fish and bread for the hungry. Watching Jesus that day must have been quite an education in miracles. It would have taught them about the power of combining gratitude with faith, and faith with broken-ness—a mixture potent enough to make a miracle. Looking back years later, they must have thought about that day on the shore in light of the last meal they ate with Jesus before his death, when his body would be broken on a Roman cross. Then too he took the bread in his hands, gave thanks, and broke it, saying, "Take and eat. This is my body."

The brokenness of Jesus is all that any of us have to offer each other. But it is that very brokenness that is the yeast for miracles. When Jesus lives in me, and I in him, then I have something to offer, no mat-ter how small my gifts. It may seem that I have so little of what others need: money, patience, time, and love. But if I take what little I do have, give thanks for it, break it open, and give it away, then I too will help feed the hungry of this world.

Jesus, when I was desperate and sick in soul, you came to me. When I was confused and alone, you took pity on me. When I was your enemy, you laid down your life for me. Your brokenness has healed me and fed me and brought peace to my soul. And now you live within me by the power of your Spirit. When I am overwhelmed by the needs of others, wondering what I can do to help, let me remember the miracle of the loaves and fishes. Grant that I might be a small loaf that you take in your hands, break open, and hand out to those who are hungry.

A Miracle of Soup and Bread

By this time it was late in the day, so his [Jesus'] disciples came to him. "This is a remote place," they said, "and it's already very late. Send the people away so they can go to the surrounding countryside and villages and buy themselves something to eat." But he answered, "You give them something to eat." (MARK 6:35–37)

Paul Thigpen attended Yale University in the early seventies, an era disdainful of the supernatural. Faith was an anachronism and miracles were merely the by-product of an overactive imagination. Given time, you could find a natural explanation for anything and everything that happened. Paul himself had been an atheist for six of his teenage years, and he too had thought that matter and energy were all that existed in the universe. But that all changed with his conversion to Christian faith at the end of his senior year of high school and a subsequent two-year stint on the mission field in Europe.

At Yale, Paul was a religious studies major. One of his religion courses, taught by a skeptical professor, seemed designed to destroy rather than nourish faith. At one point, his professor made a remark about the gospel account of the multiplication of the loaves and fishes that Paul would never forget. The instructor casually noted that the account was obviously not historical because everyone knew, of course, that miracles don't happen and that food can't actually be multiplied.

"I just shook my head," remembered Paul, "and thought about the remarkable things I had experienced on the mission field during the previous two years. Before my time in Europe, that kind of remark would have corroded my faith. But now it merely sounded presumptuous and foolish.

"As a missionary, I had lived in a little town called Nieder-Woellstadt, just north of Frankfurt, Germany, on staff at a training center for Christian youths.

"Before long, word got out to backpacking tourists that we would sometimes provide free meals to those who dropped by. We often had last-minute dinner guests, but we didn't have much money for groceries. So we did what we could and hoped for the best. On a couple of occasions, the cook whispered to me: 'Paul, we just don't have enough soup and bread. Pray that God will either multiply the food or shrink our appetites.' So we prayed, and the food never ran out. The more times this happened, the more we wondered whether God was performing a miracle in our own small kitchen.

"Curiosity got the better of the two of us, so we decided to experiment. One day, we carefully measured the amount of soup in the pot and then measured how much of it we served. All the while, we watched to make sure that nobody poured water into the soup to thin it out and make it last longer. After dinner, we realized that our suspicions were true. We had, indeed, ladled out more soup than we had made.

"In addition to soup, we often served the kind of thick-crusted dark bread that is so popular in Germany. I decided to repeat the experiment. One night when our bread supply didn't match our needs for supper, I carefully measured the length of a loaf before I put it through the slicing machine. Then I reassembled it so that the slices were packed hard against each other and re-measured the bread. Just as before, the impossible had happened! The loaf was several inches longer than it had been before I sliced it.

"It's been more than twenty years since I witnessed these miracles. But they are still so vivid. I realize I can't prove anything to the world, but neither can I ignore the evidence of my own eyes."

I wonder if it takes more faith to believe that God *can* multiply food or more faith to believe that he would bother doing so. After all, why should he go to the trouble to perform a miracle simply to fill the bellies of a few hungry backpackers? Perhaps he was making a point— that the Jesus who worked miracles two thousands years ago is the same Jesus who works miracles today. Across the centuries two things have remained the same: the nature of our needs and the all-surpassing power of our God to meet them. Paul Thigpen knows that God can do whatever he wants, whenever he wants, through whomever he chooses.

Father, forgive me for the times I have tried to hem you in with my skepticism, to fashion a god after my own understanding. Open me to miracles, Lord, and give me a robust faith. Reveal you greatness, and then let me simply bow down and adore.

The Miracle of Too Many Fish

He [Jesus] said to Simon, "Put out into deep water, and let down the nets for a catch." Simon answered, "Master, we've worked hard all night and haven't caught anything. But because you say so, I will let down the nets." When they had done so, they caught such a large number of fish that their nets began to break. (LUKE 5:4–6)

Everyone knew that the best time to fish was at night. Simon Peter had been at it for hours with nothing to show for his labors. As the morning sun crept over the hills and skimmed across the Sea of Galilee, he decided he might as well dock the boat and hope for better luck tomorrow. As he was cleaning his nets, the man called Jesus decided to use his boat for a pulpit, asking Peter to put out a little from shore so he would have a better vantage point from which to address the crowd. Peter liked this Jesus. The rabbi had been to his home and prayed for his mother-in-law, who had been suffering from a high fever. He was unlike any teacher he had ever heard, telling story after story that seemed to turn the world and everything in it upside down.

Suddenly Peter realized that Jesus was talking to him. "Put out into deep water, and let down the nets for a catch." Peter respected the man as a teacher, but what did he know about fishing? He and his crew had worked hard through the night and had caught nothing. Still, he did as Jesus asked. Though he knew it to be an exercise in futility, Peter gave the signal to drop the nets and then slowly to raise them. His muscles straining as he heaved and pulled on the ropes, it seemed to

Peter as though he were attempting to raise the floor of the sea itself. At last, the nets surfaced, bulging and tearing, unable to contain so many fish. Peter called frantically to his partners to bring their boat alongside to help harvest the catch. The boats were heaped so high with fish that they began to sink.

Peter was overwhelmed by the miracle, not because of his good fortune, but because of what he was beginning to realize about the one who worked the miracle. He fell at Jesus' knees, begging him to leave him. "I am a sinful man, Lord, not fit to be in your presence." But Jesus merely said, "Don't be afraid; from now on you will catch men."

Peter had worked hard through an entire evening with nothing at all to show for his efforts. It was precisely at that point that Jesus chose to perform a miracle, and Peter himself was caught in the net that Jesus cast forth. Later, he would lead many into the early church, thus fulfilling Jesus' words about him. The most Peter had been hoping for that day was a good catch of fish to supply the morning's market. But Jesus had bigger plans. By calling Peter and the other disciples, he was weaving a net to catch the souls of countless men and women through the ages.

Lord, I sometimes forget that I can do nothing of any significance without you. All my labors, my worrying, my staying up late, and getting up early will get me nowhere if you are not leading me. Help me to remember that you alone are the one who can make me fruitful. Whenever I am tempted to limit your work in and through me, remind me of the too-many fish in the too-few nets, and help me to cast my nets when and where you say to.

A Miracle and Money

Give, and it will be given to you. A good measure, pressed down, shaken together and running over, will be poured into your lap. For with the measure you use, it will be measured to you. (LUKE 6:38)

Five dollars is a fortune if you don't have much money in your pocket. Debbi Moore had just enough for groceries that day. Family finances had been especially pinched lately, and she always shopped with cash. That way, she would be certain not to spend even a nickel more than she could afford.

On her way to the supermarket, she noticed a disheveled man standing by the side of the road. He wasn't begging for money, but only holding a sign that read, "Jesus Heals a Broken Heart." Debbi wasn't sure why, but she experienced an overwhelming urge to give him something, though she could little afford it.

She reached into the glove compartment of her car and drew out a five dollar bill. "It seemed like a lot to me," she explained, "but I knew I should give it to him. Still, I had a little problem . . . I can look you dead in the eye, aim a Frisbee at you, and hit fifty yards to your left. I wasn't sure how I was going to get the money to the man on the sidewalk. The light was turning, and I knew the cars behind me might suck the bill under their wheels. So I said, 'This one's for you, Lord. You've got to get it there.' Then I crumpled it up and threw it out the passenger window. As I drove past, a glance in my side mirror showed the man's foot on the five dollar bill.

"After that I forgot all about it. But the next night I attended a prayer meeting and someone handed me an envelope. Inside was a gift certificate for twenty dollars to a local grocery store. In front of the certificate was a crisp five dollar bill!"

That day, Debbi Moore made an investment that Wall Street would kill for. She got a four hundred percent return on her money in less than forty-eight hours. Though Debbi didn't give because she was expecting anything in return, the gift in the envelope confirmed her belief that it is impossible to outdo the generosity of God.

Her story brings to mind the counsel of Jesus himself: "Give, and it will be given to you. A good measure, pressed down, shaken together and running over, will be poured into your lap. For with the measure you use, it will be measured to you." But Jesus wasn't just talking about money. Before making this statement, reported in the Gospel of Luke, he says that if we don't want to be judged, we should refrain from judging, and if we want to be forgiven, then we should forgive others. The point is to be as generous as possible in our dealings with others—to show mercy, to go the extra mile, to give the benefit of the doubt, to extend a helping hand. It's not complicated, it's simply living out the Golden Rule in everyday terms.

Lord, living life on spiritual terms isn't nearly as complex as I sometimes make it. In essence, it simply means obeying your two great commands: to love you with all my heart, soul, and mind, and to love others as myself. Help me to keep these two things constantly in focus and let every other concern recede into the background.

The Miracle of Oil

❧

Elisha said [to the widow], "Go around and ask all your neighbors for empty jars. Don't ask for just a few. Then go inside and shut the door behind you and your sons. Pour oil into all the jars, and as each is filled, put it to one side." (2 KINGS 4:3–5)

Once upon a time in Ancient Israel, there was a poor widow whose creditors were threatening to take her two sons as slaves if she didn't pay her husband's debts. Back then, you couldn't keep your creditors at bay simply by declaring bankruptcy. It was pay up or put up. And it looked like the latter, until the prophet Elisha came to the rescue.

It seems that the widow's husband had been in the same line of work as Elisha. So it was to Elisha she went with her troubles. As soon as he heard of her dilemma, he asked how he could help. "What do you have in your house?" he probed.

"Your servant has nothing at all," she said, "except a little oil." That's when he told her to start knocking on doors to collect all the jars she could get her hands on. So she and her sons did just that. Then he told her to start pouring the oil into the jars. She poured and she poured and she poured some more until every jar was filled to the brim. It wasn't until the very last jar had been topped off that she ran out of oil.

Now in those days the kind of oil you had in your kitchen was worth a lot of money. Since she had so much of it, the widow sold the excess, made more than enough money to pay off her debts, and she and her sons lived happily ever after. Thanks to a miracle, what little she had was more than enough to save the day.

Unlike the widow, I have never had the misfortune of being in debt up to my ears. The wolf has never stood howling at my door. And the bank has never threatened to repossess anything, not even my car. I have been greatly blessed, and I know it. But it is one thing to have money in the bank and another to have enough spiritual capital in your soul. The truth is that I often lack both the emotional and spiritual resources that seem so necessary to daily life—patience, time, perspective, energy, confidence, wisdom, understanding, forgiveness, faith, hope for the future. Perhaps you can identify with my list. Or maybe you have a list of your own.

The point of the widow's story is that God can take what little we have and multiply it if we will ask and have faith. Elisha encouraged the widow to exercise her faith by requiring her to borrow as many jars as she could in which to store the oil. But when she went knocking on doors, she still had only a little oil in her possession. It was the same with Noah when God instructed him to make an ark. He had to build the boat before even a drop of water had fallen from the sky.

This doesn't mean that God will answer every one of our prayers precisely as we want him to if we will only have enough faith. He may assess our needs differently than we do, allowing some of them to go unmet or to wait awhile so that he can work out a deeper purpose in our lives.

Whatever the case, life goes much better with faith. If you feel that you have too little of this precious commodity, ask God to multiply it. And if you haven't already done so, pray for his Spirit to indwell you. Interestingly enough, oil is actually a symbol for the Holy Spirit.

And it is the Spirit who gives us life, enabling us to have faith in a God who will meet our deepest needs, no matter how impossibly desperate we feel.

Father, thank you for the new day. For the sun that scatters red and green and gold across the earth to make our world beautiful. For the trees that keep the soil from blowing away and the hills that make life interesting. For the fuel in our stoves, the food on our table, and the hope in our hearts. For one another. For your Spirit. We thank you. Help us to be glad for all that you have given. And so increase our faith for all that you intend to give us still.

Four

Miracles and Angels

It would seem, then, that when a number of the faithful meet together genuinely for the glory of Christ . . . each of them will have, encamped beside him, his own angel, whom God has appointed to guard him and care for him. So when the saints are assembled, there will be a double Church, one of men and one of angels.
—ORIGEN

*A*ngels are the entourage of God. Wherever they are at work, you will find traces of the divine. No wonder we find them so fascinating.

Still, I wonder how these powerful creatures feel when they see images of themselves pinned to our lapels, pasted on bumper stickers, or printed on gift wrap. Recently a friend showed me a delightful cartoon depicting a scene in heaven. A crowd of angels were standing in a heavenly courtroom all clamoring for God's attention. Adorned with the stereotypical white beard, God faced them, gavel in hand, trying to restore order to the court. The caption read: "Now I don't want to hear anymore about the royalties you've been missing from all those angel books!" The angels could get rich on our devotion.

Our love affair with them may stem from the fact that we crave protection, love, and beauty. How encouraging to think that beautiful beings watch over us in the midst of a dangerous and violent world. Angels open us to wonder. They lighten our burdens. They convince us that good does triumph over evil. If we let them, they soften our unbelief and draw back the veil between the natural and the supernatural. More than that, they teach us something about the character of God.

If we find the angels dazzling, how much more should we bow down and adore the one they call "Master." For he is the fountainhead of power, beauty, mercy, loving kindness, and all joy.

Take a few moments to think about the angels and then thank God for giving you such wonderful and powerful protectors. Tell him how glad you are to belong to him, and then worship him with all your heart.

The Angel and the Accident

If you make the Most High your dwelling—even the Lord, who is my refuge—then no harm will befall you. . . . For he will command his angels concerning you to guard you in all your ways; they will lift you up in their hands, so that you will not strike your foot against a stone. (PSALM 91:9–12)

Sharyl Smith was a student nurse who had a reputation for queasiness. She had walked out, passed out, and been dragged out of operating rooms because she couldn't stand the sight and smells of surgery. You wouldn't have pegged her as a hero at the scene of a gory accident. But she was.

Her story appears in the summer 1993 issue of *The Journal of Christian Nursing.* She was on her way to school when she rounded a hill in her car. In the line of traffic ahead she saw a large truck crossing an intersection. Suddenly it appeared to " break apart, like a train derailing." Pieces of it caught fire and landed on the side of the road ahead of her. Sharyl pulled over. The cab had tumbled into a ditch, and she could see the driver slumped over the steering wheel, a wash of blood obscuring his face.

She screamed for help, but people stood paralyzed, gaping at the wreck. Someone shouted that the truck was about to explode. Then she saw it. Gasoline was gushing out of the tank onto the ground. The cab was already on fire and so was the grass in the ditch. She hesitated for a moment and then ran toward the truck.

"If no one would help me, then I'd just have to get him out alone. I would rather die than stand there and watch that man die. As I ran through the fire to the truck, I felt as though an invisible bubble was wrapped around me, protecting me. When I opened the cab door, fire shot out toward me, yet I was not burned. The ruptured gas tank poured gasoline toward my feet, making a strange sound as it poured onto the ground."

Terrified lest the truck blow up, she dragged the limp body of the man partly out of the cab. His pants were already on fire, but she couldn't seem to pull him clear of the wreck. Desperately, she prayed, "Dear God, please help us!"

Suddenly a man appeared at her side. The driver's foot had been lodged in the door, and he lifted it free. Then he smothered the remaining flames on the injured man's clothes, and together they dragged him to safety.

By then the police had arrived with an ambulance. At the hospital, Sharyl was given some scrubs to change into. As she removed the white ivory cross from her neck, she realized it was covered with blood. Alone in the room, she opened the window wide, gazed out at the blue sky, and thanked God for his mercy.

Against all odds she was alive and so was the driver of that ill-fated truck. Later, she learned that he had made a full recovery.

Sharyl knows there was more to it than one woman's act of bravery. "I have no explanation for the bubble of protection that I felt while in the fiery ditch. I know the soles of my rubber shoes were melted; flames shot out of the cab directly toward my head when I opened the door; not one hair on my head was even singed, not one burn did I acquire. I am convinced that God sent an angel to protect me that fateful day. . . . I do not know why the accident happened. . . . I only know that I believe in divine intervention. I believe in miracles."

Jesus, after two thousand years, your words still haunt us: "Greater love has no one than this, that he lay down his life for his friends." Give us the courage to live them, no matter the cost.

Three Angels to the Rescue

When you walk through the fire, you will not be burned; the flames will not set you ablaze. For I am the Lord, your God, the Holy One of Israel, your Savior. (ISAIAH 43:2–3)

Roseanne Koskie didn't have a clue that November 10, 1993, would be different than any other day. If she had, she might have chosen to stay in bed that morning.

"I drive a '91 Plymouth Acclaim," she explained. "It never gave me any trouble until the day a coworker and I decided to have lunch at Grandy's, a restaurant on the east side of El Paso. Over lunch we discussed business and then prepared to leave. But there was only one problem. My car wouldn't start.

"I tried the ignition again, but nothing happened. The engine wouldn't turn over. My friend, Sandy, suggested I give it some gas, but I explained that this was a fuel-injected engine. I didn't need to press the accelerator for the cylinders to fire. But try as I might, the car wouldn't start. Since we were parked on an incline, we began to wonder if somehow fuel wasn't getting through the line. Perhaps it needed a little extra oomph to get things moving. So I pumped the pedal a couple of times. But still, nothing happened. At that point, Sandy offered to go back into the restaurant to call for help.

"I sat in the car for a minute, when suddenly, I noticed what looked like flames flicking from under the hood. It couldn't be fire, I thought. The engine never even started. Without thinking, I got out of the car and raised the hood. Sure enough, the front of the car was on fire. I ran to the trunk for a blanket to smother the flames, but as I raced back to the front of the car, I knew there would be no putting this fire out. Not by me anyway.

"The flames seemed to grow larger each second. I stood there mesmerized, staring into the fire. I couldn't seem to move. At one point I heard a voice shouting, 'Lady, get out of there! It's going to explode!' But still I couldn't find my feet. Suddenly, I felt someone grab me by the shoulders, pulling me away from the car to safety. I looked around to see who it was, but no one was there. Then I saw two men running toward the car from different directions, both carrying fire extinguishers. Together, they doused the fire and that was the end of it.

"The car took a month to repair but both Sandy and I were safe. I discovered later that the fuel injection tube had burst, probably the moment I had pushed the pedal to the floor. We thanked God that we escaped the car when we did and that the two men just 'happened' to be in the vicinity, both with fire extinguishers and the nerve to use them. Most of all, I was grateful for invisible hands that had pulled me clear of the fire. When people ask me who it was, I tell them it was my angel. I have little doubt that God had put my guardian angel on special alert that day."

Lord, I thank you for all the times you have protected and watched over me even when I didn't know I needed watching. When I am tempted to be anxious or afraid, help me to remember your faithfulness, realizing that your mercies are new every morning and that your grace is sufficient for each day.

A Better Gift Than Angels

"Sir," the invalid replied [to Jesus], "I have no one to help me into the pool when the water is stirred. While I am trying to get in, someone else goes down ahead of me." Then Jesus said to him, "Get up! Pick up your mat and walk." At once the man was cured; he picked up his mat and walked. (JOHN 5:7–8)

On the east side of Jerusalem were mineral springs that seemed to possess healing properties. Known as the pool of Bethesda, the disabled were attracted to it as iron to a magnet. The name, Bethesda, means "house of mercy" or "house of compassion." The blind, the lame, and the paralyzed would spend day after day lying beside the pool, hoping that this would be the day they would be cured. The Jews believed that an angel of the Lord would come down from heaven to stir up the waters of the pool. The first person to enter the water once it moved, was invariably healed.

Now Jesus was walking through the area one Sabbath and noticed a man lying near the pool. This man had been an invalid for thirty-eight years. When Jesus asked him whether he wanted to be well, the man assured him that he did, though he had no one to help him enter the water once it began to stir. Then Jesus simply told him to stand, pick up his mat, and walk away. And the man did just that, to everyone's astonishment.

It's interesting to reflect on the man's experience. He must have felt lonely and at a disadvantage. The others had friends and family who could help them get into the pool quickly. But he had no one. His painstaking efforts to drag himself to the pool were always too little, too late. He was never in the right place at the right time to obtain the miracle he desired. Despite these disadvantages, he must still have had hope, for he persisted in coming to the pool. As it turned out, his hope was rewarded, though not in the way he had envisioned.

No one lifted him up, walked over to the pool, and dipped his broken body into the healing waters. Instead, Jesus uttered a simple word of command to put him on his feet again.

Like the invalid at Bethesda, you may be feeling that you are overdue for a miracle. You may have heard stories of people who have traveled across the world to some holy place or who have been prayed with by someone who is said to possesses healing powers. You wonder if it's simply a matter of being in the right place at the right time. Like the paralytic, you may feel that you have no one whose prayers will move you closer to a miracle. If so, take heart from this man's story. Despite the long delay, he still hoped that God would have mercy on him. And God did. Rather than sending an angel to heal him, He sent His only Son, a better gift than angels.

Lord, my faith is no faith at all if it depends upon whether or not you perform a miracle for me or for someone I love. And yet I believe that miracles do happen. So I ask you to look with compassion on my prayer and to grant the desires of my heart. Whether your answer is yes or no, now or later, I trust that you hear me, that you understand my distress, and that you will act with compassion.

The Little Girl and the Angel

❧❧❧

One day Jesus was praying in a certain place. When he finished, one of his disciples said to him, "Lord, teach us to pray, just as John taught his disciples." (LUKE 11:1)

One of June Scouten's favorite prayers is "The Lord's Prayer," the same one Jesus taught his disciples two thousand years ago. When you hear her story, you'll know why.

"I was six years old when it happened. My family attended a Methodist church in Washington, D.C., and one of the requirements in my Sunday school class was to learn the Lord's Prayer. I was good at a lot of things, but memorization wasn't one of them. My mother could remember anything she put her mind to, so she couldn't understand why it was so hard for me. In fact, I've always been that way. I could ad lib my way out of any kind of trouble, but couldn't memorize a page of text to save my life. No matter how hard I tried to remember the prayer, I couldn't keep the words straight.

"Saturday night came and I still couldn't recite the prayer all the way through. I was worried because I wanted to do well, but how could I? As I was climbing into bed, I said: 'God I need some help remembering this prayer. Please do something.' I drifted off into the most wonderful dream. Someone very beautiful came into my room and took me in his arms. I felt him lifting me and then transporting me through the air to a strange place. All the while, I felt safe and warm, not at all frightened by the experience. I remember seeing light, pretty colors and then being brought into the presence of someone else. Then I began to feel very small and thought to myself that I was in the presence of a Great One. Don't ask me why I thought that, I just did. Yet I still felt very much at peace. Then this person, I believe it was Jesus, spoke to me. He simply said the Lord's Prayer very deliberately and clearly one time through. Then I woke up.

"From that moment, I knew the prayer perfectly. I felt relieved and at peace, knowing I would be able to recite it at church. I don't know why God heard the prayer of a worried little girl, but I believe he sent an angel to me that night to bring me into his presence so he could teach me the prayer of his heart."

Our Father who art in heaven, hallowed be thy name. Thy kingdom come, thy will be done, on earth as it is in heaven. Give us this day our daily bread and forgive us our trespasses as we forgive those who trespass against us. Lead us not into temptation, but deliver us from evil. For thine is the kingdom, the power, and the glory both now and forever. Amen.

An Angel on an Airplane

&c&o&

Are not all angels ministering spirits sent to serve those who will inherit salvation? (HEBREWS 1:14)

Gloria Thompson worked in the sales division of a large firm in the Southwest. A seasoned traveler, she spent many hours in airplanes crisscrossing the country. In the course of her travels, she'd had some interesting encounters with fellow passengers but nothing like the one she was about to experience that Friday in October of 1995.

She had just boarded a flight bound for Detroit, when a middle-aged man took his seat beside her. Her gaze rested on him only for an instant, but she had the impression that the man was deeply troubled, despite the smile on his face. She breathed a silent prayer, asking that God would protect him from the temptation to commit suicide. "This is crazy," she thought. "I don't even know the guy. Still, I guess it doesn't hurt to pray."

The plane was about to depart, when he turned and asked whether this was the flight to Duluth. Startled, she replied that it was the flight to Detroit, Michigan, not Duluth, Minnesota. She advised him to check with a flight attendant immediately if he thought he had walked onto the wrong flight. But the man seemed paralyzed by confusion. He explained that he had accepted a job as a regional sales rep for a firm he thought was located in Duluth. But maybe it was in Detroit. He wasn't sure. He pulled out his ticket, which was written for

Detroit. A quick phone call to his new company confirmed that he was on the right flight.

Clearly, the man had problems. He introduced himself as Dick and began to talk freely, perhaps thinking she needed an explanation for his confused behavior. Years earlier, he was diagnosed as being bipolar. He had what was commonly known as manic depression. Now he was at his wits end. He hadn't eaten in four days and had nowhere to live and no money to live on. His family in Dallas had refused to bail him out one more time, so frustrated were they by his behavior. Somehow he had landed a job with the firm in Detroit, and they had agreed to fly him in for a few days of orientation. He would have to pay his travel expenses out of his first paycheck. Still, he was uncertain whether to accept the job. Past experience had told him that his depression and anxiety cycled out of control whenever he spent long hours alone on the road, which was exactly what was required in the new job. His therapist had counseled him to remain in Dallas. But he had spurned that advice because living in Dallas would have meant entering a shelter for homeless men. He knew he was running away from his problems, but he felt trapped and desperate. He had never felt so hopeless and afraid as he did that night on the flight to Detroit.

As they talked, he admitted that he had entertained thoughts of suicide. Maybe that would finally put an end to his torment. Gloria spoke with Dick for the duration of the flight and tried to encourage him as best she could. When he asked whether she thought he ought to seek emergency counseling in Detroit, she agreed to help him. He seemed incapable of making a decision on his own. She had planned to spend the weekend with her family, who lived in the area, prior to a week full of meetings in the city. But she knew she could be flexible about her schedule that Friday night, especially if it meant helping someone in trouble.

It took a few hours to get Dick the kind of help he needed. But she was glad she'd made the effort. On the advice of crisis counselors, he committed himself to a psychiatric hospital in the area, where he received medication to help control his depression and anxiety. In the week that followed, Gloria stayed in touch by phone and visited him in the psychiatric hospital, before returning to her home in Colorado. She was surprised that the hospital staff knew all about her and that the nurses kept telling Dick he had angels watching out for him.

Dick stayed in Detroit for a month. While he was there, two of Gloria's brothers did their best to befriend him. They spent hours talking with him, encouraging him to face his problems. Reluctantly, Dick returned to Dallas to face the music. When he did, one of his brothers met him at the bus station. With the help of his brother and a friend who lent him some money to help him back on his feet, Dick was able to find a place to live, which was decidedly better than being out on the street.

Since then, Dick and Gloria have spoken on the phone several times. Not surprisingly, Dick has had his ups and downs. Gloria knows he isn't out of the woods by any stretch of the imagination. Though she doesn't know whether Dick will be able to turn his life around, she hopes he has at least turned an important corner. Of one thing she is certain, though: God has turned a needy stranger into a friend for whom she will continue to pray.

When Gloria returned home from her trip to Detroit, she thought about what had happened on the plane that day. She had prayed for a stranger, not knowing that God would invite her and her two brothers to become part of the answer to that prayer. Later, when she visited

Dick in the psychiatric ward before returning home, she noticed that he wore a small angel pin on the collar of his shirt. When Dick explained that a passenger on the previous flight had given it to him, she couldn't help but smile. Wasn't it just like God to send a token of his love! No matter what Dick would face in the days and months ahead, she knew that heavenly protectors wouldn't be far away.

Father, I'm amazed that you weave us into the fabric of your miracles. So often, you funnel your help through us, rather than pushing us aside to accomplish your purposes. As we intercede, may we be willing to become part of the answer to our prayer for others, no matter how hopeless the situation. Ultimately, Lord, the outcome is in your hands.

Five

Miracles of Life
and Death

There are only two ways to live your life. One is as though nothing is a miracle. The other is as if everything is.
—ALBERT EINSTEIN

When I was a child, someone gave me an unusual necklace. It was a round globe of glass attached to a silver chain. Inside the glass was a small seed. I loved peering at the seed, wondering how it got trapped inside the glass. But to tell the truth, I would have liked it even better had the glass encased something really interesting—like a bumble bee or a mosquito. I didn't realize that my new bauble was supposed to remind me of the words of Jesus: "I tell you the truth, if you have faith as small as a mustard seed, you can say to this mountain, 'Move from here to there' and it will move. Nothing will be impossible for you."

But what are these mountains Jesus speaks of? Is he encouraging us to start rearranging the surrounding landscape, moving mountains as we would the furniture in our living rooms? Somehow I doubt it. Instead, I think he is saying that even the tiniest amount of faith can create spiritual earthquakes. These earthquakes sometimes happen in families, where one person prays for the conversion of the rest. Or in communities, where different individuals are touched by God's power and his love. Sometime they involve matters of life and death, and at other times they shake things up more gradually and quietly.

If you know of particular mountains that need moving, remember the role that faith plays. As you read the stories that follow, I hope they will strengthen the faith you already have so that you, too, will experience a miracle in your life.

A Death-Defying Miracle

"Take away the stone," he said. "But, Lord," said Martha, the sister of the dead man, "by this time, there is a bad odor, for he has been there four days." Then Jesus said, "Did I not tell you that if you believed, you would see the glory of God?" So they took away the stone.... Jesus called in a loud voice, "Lazarus, come out!" The dead man came out, his hands and feet wrapped with strips of linen, and a cloth around his face. Jesus said to them, "Take off the grave clothes and let him go." (JOHN 11:39–40, 43–44)

I came face to face with death for the first time when I was nine years old. And I didn't like what I saw. My father's mother had died and we arrived at the funeral home to pay our respects. Shortly after we got there, I saw my grandfather lean over the casket and kiss my grandmother, lying so still and pale. I suppose it was a tender moment, but it frightened me. Someone asked whether I would like to kiss her, but I said no. The thick make-up spread over her skin only made her look gray and cold as a stone. The best I could do was recite a quiet prayer in front of her casket.

The next day, we arrived at my grandfather's house before the funeral. As soon as I walked through the door, I was struck speechless. There on the couch sat my grandmother, fifty pounds lighter, but full of life! I could hear her voice again, recognize the familiar gesture as she flicked the too-long ashes from her cigarette. Her skin looked pink and fresh and soft against her raven hair. But before I could rush over and throw my arms around her, someone introduced her as my Great Aunt Leonore. I hadn't even known my grandmother had a sister, let alone one that looked just like her. Of course I was glad to meet my aunt but crushed by my childish mistake. People don't rise from the dead, after all. What had I been thinking?

But I have since come to believe that sometimes people do rise from the grave. Unlike me, Martha and Mary didn't suffer a case of mistaken identity. Their brother Lazarus really had walked out of his tomb, slow and stiff, to be sure. But there was no question he was alive again.

Still, they had doubted Jesus for the miracle. Mary had thrown herself at Jesus' feet, weeping because he had arrived too late to heal her brother. And Martha had balked when he ordered the stone removed from the tomb. "Lord, don't you realize he's been dead for four days? He'll stink if you open the tomb!" But Jesus insisted and the impossible happened.

This incredible miracle is a sign of hope for every follower of Christ in every age of the church. Without the assurance that we will live forever, healing would have little value. It would only be a delaying tactic, staving off annihilation for a few moments, days, or years. Inevitably, our hearts will one-day stop, our lungs will pump their last molecule of oxygen, and our brains will be incapable of one more thought. But that won't be the end of us. Because the Spirit of Jesus dwells in us, we will hear his voice beckoning, and our last enemy, death, will finally be swallowed up by life. When that happens, I plan on sitting down beside my grandmother, throwing my arms around her, and telling her just how glad I am to see her.

Jesus, it's no wonder Mary and Martha had a hard time believing. But all you asked was that they have enough faith to roll away the stone from the tomb. Please forgive my skepticism and remove the stone of unbelief from my heart. When the time comes, grant me the grace of a peaceful death.

The Miracle of a Happy Death

Precious in the sight of the Lord is the death of his saints. (PSALM 116:15)

Are not two sparrows sold for a penny? Yet not one of them will fall to the ground apart from the will of your Father. And even the very hairs of your head are all numbered. So don't be afraid; you are worth more than many sparrows. (MATTHEW 10:29–31)

Joan Lindeman and her husband, Don, lived in Almond, New York. They had been married forty years, but their time together was drawing to a close. Six months earlier, Don had tentatively been diagnosed with Alzheimer's disease. The prognosis was horrifying. In Joan's mind, the future loomed like a living death sentence for him. Alive in body but so far away in spirit.

Joan's sense of loss was sharpened by the fact that one of her sons had been killed just two weeks before she moved Don into a nursing home twenty miles away. Every afternoon she made the trip to see him. Tears salted her prayers as she crossed and recrossed the twenty miles that separated them. Knowing that Alzheimer's patients often live for many years, she cried out to God, asking him to spare Don from this long misery. "The day he doesn't know me, will be the saddest day of my life," she thought.

"One morning I was speaking to my son who lives in Florida. He knew the stress I had been under and would call frequently to see how his dad and I were faring. It was such a comfort to talk with him that we would usually chat for a half hour or more. But shortly after he called, I had an irresistible urge to hang up and leave for the nursing home. As soon as I put the phone down, my daughter-in-law called. She was still grieving the loss of her husband, my other son. I was so aware of her pain that I hated to cut her short, but I just knew I had to get to the nursing home. 'This doesn't make any sense,' I thought to myself. 'Don was fine when I left him yesterday. But I'm sure he needs me.'

"As soon as I arrived, a nurse hailed me. Donald was ill. The doctor who had just examined him couldn't explain why his temperature had suddenly spiked. Perhaps he was struggling with a bout of the flu.

"I rushed into his room, shocked to see my husband lying in bed, his face the color of bleached linen and glistening with sweat. Without a word, he grasped my hand and looked into my eyes for reassurance. I spoke lovingly to him, patting the moisture from his face. Then he died in my arms.

"Had I ignored the feeling that he needed me, I would have missed the chance to be with Don when he died. It was heartbreaking to lose him, but I was comforted by the thought that his sufferings had been brief and that we had been together the moment he left this earth. The doctors had thought he would live for many years, but God, in his mercy, had other plans. By some miracle of divine radar, God let me tune in to what was happening so that I could be there when Don needed me most."

Father, death is never easy. Often it is an ugly and painful experience. Frightening for those who die and for those who are left behind. But it comforts me to know that you do not abandon us when it's time to pass from this world to the next. You mark the moment with your mercy, assuring us that we are of more value to you than we can possibly imagine. Give us, we ask, a death that is full of both your peace and your presence.

A Child's Miracle

"For I know the plans I have for you," declares the Lord, "plans to prosper you and not to harm you, plans to give you hope and a future." (JEREMIAH 29:11)

It was 1955. Dr. Jonas Salk was the man of the year in America. His miracle vaccine was about to put an end to the terror that stalked the world's children, crippling or killing hundreds of thousands of children during each successive epidemic. Thanks to Salk, polio would soon become as rare in the developed world as the bubonic plague. Millions of children across the United States would be the first to benefit.

Unfortunately, Marilyn Graven Smith wasn't one of them. The child of American missionaries, she was excitedly awaiting Christmas at home in Phnom Penh, Cambodia. Neither she nor her parents had the slightest hint of the anguish they would endure in the next few days.

"I was sitting in the living room one Monday night when my neck suddenly began to stiffen up. It was so tight I couldn't even move it. My head ached, I was feverish, and when I tried to talk, the words tumbled out in a slur. On Tuesday, my father took me to our family doctor, who immediately admitted me to the hospital. He suspected polio, but tried to soften the blow by saying that it might be meningitis.

"On Wednesday morning a French specialist, who was touring Asia to study the outbreak of polio, stopped by to see me and later confirmed the diagnosis. It was bulbar polio.

"Simultaneously, the field chairman for the mission wired the national office in New York, asking people to pray for ten-year-old Marilyn Graven, who wasn't expected to live. Telegrams flew across continents and people throughout the world begged God for a miracle.

"By Wednesday night my right side was paralyzed from the neck down and no one could understand a word of what I said. I didn't know it, but when I went to sleep that night, none of the hospital staff expected me to wake up the next day.

"When my doctor walked into my room Thursday morning, he was astonished to see me sitting up in bed, talking a blue streak in much-improved English. As a further test, he asked me to get out of bed and walk to the door. I was so eager to prove I was well that I ran across the room and nearly toppled over in the process. Of course I was still weak from the last few days, but the paralysis had definitely disappeared.

"My family doctor was an agnostic, but when Dad asked him whether my recovery was a miracle, he simply shook his head and replied, 'Without doubt, without doubt.' Word of my case soon spread throughout Southeast Asia. I had survived a terrible killer through the power of prayer.

"I knew with certainty that God had saved my life that night. The child of missionaries, I was often asked by well-meaning adults whether I planned to become one when I grew up. My answer was always swift and definite. The last thing I would ever be was a missionary. I didn't even want to consider it. But when God healed me, I realized the future wasn't entirely mine to decide. He had kept me alive for a reason. Somehow I knew he had a plan for my life, and I didn't want to miss it. Before long, I started to warm to the idea of missionary work. Eventually, I ended up serving with my husband in Peru and Ecuador."

Marilyn Graven was a fortunate little girl. Through the mercy of a loving God and the power of prayer, polio was robbed of one of its victims. Her story reminds us that no matter how desperate our present circumstances, God himself cups the future in his hands.

Father, you hold the world and all its children within your grasp. You created each of us from nothing, and you love the work of your hands. When we are tempted to despair, let us remember that you are the Lord of both life and death. Not even a sparrow falls to the ground without your knowing it. With that assurance, let us surrender to the future, believing that whether we live or whether we die, you will keep us safe.

A Miracle of Hope

May the God of hope fill you with all joy and peace as you trust in him, so that you may overflow with hope by the power of the Holy Spirit. (ROMANS 15:13)

Brad and Judy Fletcher had decided to move to a larger city from a rural community twenty-five miles away. "We made an offer on a house three doors down from our friends, Bob and Liz," Brad explained, "but the deal fell through because our house was slow to sell. Meanwhile, someone else bought the home we had hoped to move into. But Liz and Judy wouldn't give up. On the Fourth of July, they passed out fliers in the neighborhood advertising our interest. When they passed 3612 Frederick St., Judy stopped for a moment and said, 'that's the house were supposed to have. I don't know how I know, but I do.'

"One Saturday in September we received a surprise call from the owners of that home. Sure enough the second sale had fallen through. Had our house sold yet? It had and we were interested. The closing date was set for October 29. Had I known then what I know now, I would have chosen a different date.

"For several months I had been working on a multimillion-dollar deal on behalf of my company. Soon I discovered that the closing date for the wire transfer of funds was also set for October 29—in Baltimore. The timing was less than ideal, but my father agreed to take my place and accompany Judy to the closing for our new home.

"The evening of October 27, Judy took our daughters, Julie and Kelly, out to dinner to celebrate. As soon as they returned home, Judy became ill with what she thought was either the flu or food poisoning. But it was something far worse. By morning she was lying on the floor vomiting. She was in so much pain that she begged God to let her die. Fortunately, a business associate stopped by the house to drop off some papers related to the closing. He became alarmed when he saw Judy and called me in Baltimore. I spoke to Judy on the phone and could tell that something was terribly wrong with her. She was disoriented and didn't seem to know what was going on. We arranged for her to get to the hospital immediately, and I left to catch the first plane home.

"I braced myself as I entered the hospital. For a moment, I felt as though I had accidentally stepped onto a movie set in the middle of its most tragic scene. The family was in tears. A social worker was there to help prepare the girls for the worst. And it seemed the hospital staff was trying to keep the patient alive until her husband arrived to spend precious last minutes alone with his wife.

"Judy's doctor explained that she was in a coma and on life support. She went into respiratory arrest while she was being examined in the emergency room. Had she arrived a few minutes later, we would have already been discussing the funeral. The diagnosis was spinal meningitis. She had hydrocephalus, which was putting enormous pressure on her brain. He had inserted shunts to relieve the pressure and was hoping antibiotics would control the infection.

"I had served in a medical intensive care unit during my stint in the navy. When I entered Judy's room for the first time, I couldn't help but think that some of the people we had lost in that unit looked better than she did.

"Afterward, I took Julie and Kelly to the chapel to pray. 'Kids, your mother is going to live, although we don't know where yet. She will either live with us in our new home, or she will live with Jesus in heaven. Let's pray for healing, strength, and the grace to accept God's will.'

"By Saturday the doctor informed me that most patients in Judy's condition either died or suffered severe brain damage, causing minimal quality of life. He warned me that I might need to face the decision of whether to take her off life support.

"But neither I nor anyone else was willing to give up hope. Friends rented a van and moved our things into our home. Casseroles appeared on our doorstep. People showed up to rake leaves and clean house. Men and women all over the city were praying for Judy's recovery. Entire congregations were interceding and before long the Judy Fletcher prayer chain stretched across several states. Fortunately, our new home was just five minutes from the hospital, and our neighbor, Liz, became like a second mother to our daughters. God had indeed earmarked that house on Frederick Street as our new home. Our little family had never realized there was so much love in the world.

"But Judy's coma persisted. By late November, her neurosurgeon explained that he had two alternatives: he could try a drug that might stop the swelling in her brain but would probably cause her to become a permanent invalid or he could remove part of her brain to make room for more swelling, thus buying time against the disease. As someone who always carefully considers his options, I pressed hard for a third alternative. Her doctor gave it to me: 'He could do nothing, and she would die.' I chose option two.

"On Thanksgiving Day he operated, and family and friends gathered in the waiting room still praying for a miracle. In an act of faith, one of our friends, Lana, showed up with a Christmas tree, a string, and some popcorn. She put us to work making the decorations. It was her way of saying that Judy would survive the operation and that we might as well decorate the tree in preparation for Christmas. While the surgeon was in one room trying to save Judy's life, Lana was in another trying to save us from despair.

"Judy survived the operation. After forty-five days, she emerged from her coma. The Christmas season arrived, and I had the joy of seeing her lifted from bed and placed in a wheelchair for the first time since she entered the hospital. It was both a beautiful and pathetic sight. Judy looked as though she had just come in second in a bull fight. But I received the best Christmas gift anyone could ever ask for. I had the joy of wheeling my wife out of intensive care in order to show off the Christmas tree we had decorated for her on Thanksgiving.

"Before long, she was in a rehabilitation unit, though her prognosis was still dismal. But we refused to stop hoping for a total cure. By March the light at the end of the tunnel became visible. She could take a few steps without assistance, her hair had grown into a fashionable butch cut, and she could carry on a coherent conversation. To everyone's amazement, she recovered fully except for some short-term memory loss. When I asked the nurses and doctors who they thought was responsible for her cure, not one of them claimed credit. They simply pointed toward heaven when asked about her remarkable recovery.

"Finally, a hundred and fifty-five days after the onset of her illness, I took Judy home. It was Good Friday, April 1, 1988. But we immediately renamed it 'Great Friday.'"

Lord, in the midst of tragedy, we pray for the grace to hold on to two things: our hope in you and our love for one another. With these two gifts, we will taste victory, no matter what happens.

A Miracle of Life

You created my inmost being; you knit me together in my mother's womb. I praise you because I am fearfully and wonderfully made. (PSALM 139:13–14)

"I wasn't supposed to be born," explains John Drahos. "My mother was partially paralyzed and nearly totally bedridden with multiple sclerosis, when her doctor told her she was pregnant. She was delighted with the news. After three failed pregnancies, she was longing for a child.

"But her doctor was so worried that his bedside manner failed him completely. 'If you decide to carry this baby to term, you're going to have to find another doctor,' he told her. 'I'm not going to stand by and watch you give birth to a baby you can't possibly care for. Furthermore, you know as well as I do that this child might be physically or mentally handicapped. You can't take the kind of medicine you've been on, without suffering the consequences.'

"But my mother was determined: 'This child is a human being whose life I have no right to take. If it *is* malformed, then my husband and I will give it that much more love, and we will find a way to care for the baby.'

"She wouldn't budge, and so I was born. I had all ten fingers and toes, two eyes, a nose, and, according to my mother, the most beautiful smile in the world. I did suffer from some minor health problems, but soon I was as well as any normal child.

"Best of all, immediately after I was born, my mother experienced a total remission from her MS, which lasted for seven years! She was so energetic that she even chased me up and down the terraced lawns behind our house when I was young and full of mischief.

"In today's overheated debate about abortion, one rarely thinks of the issue from the child's viewpoint. That's why I'm so glad to tell my story. Were it not for my mother's reverence for human life and her courage in challenging the 'medical wisdom' of her doctor, I would never have known the intoxicating smell of a freshly cut rose, the glow of moonlight on a green lawn, or the loving touch of another human being. I would have missed the miracle that is life."

Father, because you knit us together in our mother's wombs, our lives have meaning and eternal significance. Help us to live every day conscious of the sacredness of life. As this reverence deepens, may we treat each other accordingly, with dignity and respect, with love and mercy, just as you treat us.

Six

❧

Miracles, Not Magic

Whenever, therefore, people are deceived and form opinions wide of the truth, it is clear that the error has slid into their minds through the medium of certain resemblances to that truth.
—SOCRATES

*A*t first glance, magic and miracles may seem to have a great deal in common. Both attract our attention and our wonder. Both purport to be caused by extraordinary powers beyond our reasoning. But in fact, miracles are as different from magic as the Mona Lisa is from its numerous counterfeits.

Magic, on the one hand, always seeks to dazzle. It calls attention to the skills of the magician and his supposed power over the natural world. It distracts and blinds us by its brilliance.

By contrast, Jesus never once played to the crowd's desire to be entertained or dazzled. Neither did he use his miraculous powers in a self-aggrandizing manner. At times he even took pains to silence people about the great things he had done for them. He knew that many people were only hungry for spiritual glitter, not for the deeper message of the gospel. These were the ones who would forever desert him when they realized that suffering and sacrifice were integral to his message.

Scripture makes clear that Satan himself is capable of performing signs and wonders. The Book of Revelation predicts that the satanic Antichrist will one day perform great "miracles" in the hopes of leading men and women astray. Such signs are merely stage props for a counterfeit gospel, one that appeals to our desire for power and our aversion to self-sacrifice. In the end, this is a gospel that ultimately enslaves us to evil.

It is the opposite with authentic miracles. They encourage us to embrace the whole gospel, the part that makes us uncomfortable as well as the part that attracts us. Ultimately, true wonders point to a gospel that has as its primary miracle the greatest sign of all—the one we call the sign of the cross.

If you find that you are always looking for "signs and wonders" to validate your faith, it might be time for some soul-searching. Ask God for the gift of true faith, which rests not on the action or inaction of God but on the unshakable foundation of his character and his goodness. Stop looking for something extraordinary to happen. And start looking for God to reveal himself in the ordinary events of your life.

The Miracle of Walking on Water

He [Jesus] saw the disciples straining at the oars, because the wind was against them. About the fourth watch of the night he went out to them, walking on the lake. . . . when they saw him walking on the lake, they though he was a ghost. They cried out, because they all saw him and were terrified. (MARK 6:48, 49–50)

*T*grew up with water skis on my feet. I loved the exhilarating feeling of balancing on a slalom as it beat a staccato rhythm across the water. One day, my brother and I hit upon a thrilling idea. We would try skiing barefoot! We had long admired the college kids who lived on our lake in the summer. The more daring of these would ski barefoot behind powerful boats. We decided to start with one ski and then gracefully slip out of it once the boat built up speed. But there was little grace in our attempt. As soon as we slipped out of the ski, we sunk like rocks. Instead of speeding across the waves on our own two feet, we were left eating the wake of the boat as it sped away. We hadn't realized that our little motor lacked the power to keep our skiless feet above the water.

That stormy night on Galilee, Jesus manifested a power beyond anything we can comprehend. It wasn't a sorcerer's magic over the elements but the Creator's control over his own creation. His disciples were terrified, mistaking him for a ghost. Remarkably, their frightened response comes mere hours after the miracle of the multiplication of the loaves and fishes. Their faith had grown stronger as they passed out the bread and fish, but not strong enough to match the immensity of Jesus' power.

The same is true for us. We may have seen a miracle or two. We certainly know by personal experience that God loves us and cares for us. Yet in the middle of the night, when the storm rages most fiercely, we still cry out with fear.

How did Jesus respond to the disciples' fearful cries? Did he tell them to buck up and stop being babies? No, he told them to have courage. Then he climbed into the boat and calmed the wind. And that's the way he treats us, speaking a word of courage, assuring us of his presence, and calming our souls. We may feel that we are alone on a dark night, in the middle of an angry sea, but the truth is that God sees us no matter where we are or what we are going through. Just as Jesus walked on the water to come to the disciples, he can use the very problems we experience in order to come to us and calm our fears.

Lord, my faith is so small, and your power is so great. When will I ever get this through my head—and my heart? With each year that passes, may the gap between my faith and your faithfulness decrease, so that I will actually live my life by faith rather than by sight. Meanwhile, I thank you that you comfort me and assure me of your love even when I have so little faith.

99

A Magic Act

When Jesus had called the Twelve together, he gave them power and authority to drive out all demons. (LUKE 9:1)

d Allen and his young friends were performing in the middle of a huge underground shopping mall. They were spending a few months in Europe and had formed a Christian band in the hopes of interesting other young people in the gospel. Peppered throughout the mall were all kinds of crazy acts: jugglers, magicians, you name it. Ed and his friends performed free, but most of the others passed the hat in order to put bread on the table.

"While we were taking a break from our act," Ed explained, "another friend came running towards us saying, 'You've got to come right away.' Not knowing what to expect, we followed him to another part of the shopping center. A crowd had gathered around a particularly bizarre act. We couldn't tell for sure, but the two performers looked as though they were from India. When one of the men appeared to fall into a trance the other one handed him what looked like knitting needles. The crowd gasped as the first man thrust the needles into his body with no apparent sign of pain. People were definitely impressed, but we were troubled. We knew the difference between magic and miracles. The God we believed in didn't do things just for show, nor did he require people to mutilate their bodies. There was power here all right, but it wasn't a benign form of spiritual power.

"Standing in back of the crowd, we dropped to our knees and asked God to do something. As we stood up, we saw the assistant hand the man another needle. Once again, he tried shoving it into his palm. But this time nothing happened. He tried it again with no result. Instead of penetrating his body, the needle actually bent against his bare flesh. It wouldn't go in. At this point, the assistant became agitated and shook the man out of his trance. They looked around with fear in their eyes, picked up their things and ran."

Ed and his friends had an encounter they will never forget. Clearly, some power was at work to enable the man in the trance to mutilate himself without any sign of pain or even discomfort. Yet they believed it an evil power, out to seduce the crowd, and their prayers seemed to have proved them right.

Shortly after I heard this story, I tuned in to an educational channel on television. A documentary was airing about a religious sect in a remote region of China. I couldn't help but think of Ed's story as I watched people shove needles, knives, and inch-wide saws through their mouths, cheeks, and tongues. Though they bled, they showed no sign of pain. What kind of god, I wondered, would require this kind of senseless disfigurement from his followers?

How can you tell the difference between magic and miracle? Often, the former is simply a raw display of power. It accomplishes nothing other than drawing attention to itself. Miracles, on the other hand, may display power, but it is power in the service of some greater good. Just because someone seems to possess extraordinary knowledge or power doesn't mean you should listen to them. And whether it's trickery or reality is not the point. Whatever it is, it springs from deception, which only leads to bondage.

Lord, you are the way, the truth, and the light. The more we know you, the greater our freedom. Your miracles bring hope and healing, not deception and disfigurement. From all false and deceiving spirits deliver us, and lead us into the light of your presence.

Show Me a Miracle

The Lord said to Moses and Aaron, "When Pharaoh says to you, 'Perform a miracle,' then say to Aaron, 'Take your staff and throw it down before Pharaoh,' and it will become a snake." (EXODUS 7:8–9)

A friend of my grandfather was an amateur magician. He would delight us with wonderful tricks, which he performed with seeming ease. My favorite was the trick of the broken toothpick. He would cover a toothpick with a handkerchief. Then he would ask me to take hold of the handkerchief and break the toothpick in half. That toothpick didn't have a chance. Each time, I twisted the sliver of wood back and forth with great energy, making absolutely certain it was broken. And each time, he magically produced an unbroken toothpick from under the cloth. It was easy to amaze me in those days.

The magicians in Pharaoh's court appeared to possess magic arts far more impressive than this. It began when Moses and Aaron went to Pharaoh claiming to have a message from God. Pharaoh was to free the Hebrew slaves so that they could worship their God. But why should Pharaoh believe Moses? And why should he care about Moses' God? Prove yourself, Pharaoh demanded, and show me a miracle.

So Aaron threw his staff on the ground and it turned into a snake. Then Pharaoh summoned his own magicians and ordered them to do the same. Each man threw down his staff and each staff turned into a snake. But apparently, not all these snakes were created equal. Aaron's quickly swallowed up the rest.

What wisdom are we to draw from this story? Was it merely the ancient equivalent of a game of tug of war, or does it have implications for us today? It might help to realize that the staff, or rod, in Scripture is often an emblem of divine power. And the serpent is a symbol of Satan. In this initial contest between Moses and Pharaoh, the authority of God establishes itself over the trickery and evil power of Satan. Pharaoh's magicians did seem to possess some kind of supernatural power. But they were no match for the greater power of God.

How fitting that Moses and Aaron should win this first contest with their enemy. Perhaps their victory was meant as much to encourage them as to frighten Pharaoh. After all, how could two nobodies challenge the power of the vast Egyptian Empire and live to tell about it?

The same contest between God and Satan rages today. Evil authorities seek to enslave people to their own sin and to the sins of others. A man abandons his lover when he discovers she is pregnant, a politician is indicted for stealing taxpayers' money, a child is abused, a wife cheats on her husband, a religious leader demonizes his enemies. Our sins are too egregious to ignore. And yet Jesus stands ready with his power to free us. We have but to ask him and then to do whatever he tells us.

Father, you desire our freedom even more than we do. Hear the cry of the weak and the oppressed. Be moved to pity by what you see. Stretch out your hand and draw us out of the grasp of evil. Bring us, then, into the promised land of your presence, where we will know what it means to be truly free.

Miracles Do Happen

Now for some time a man named Simon had practiced sorcery in the city and amazed all the people of Samaria. He boasted that he was someone great, and all the people, both high and low, gave him their attention and exclaimed, "This man is the divine power known as the Great Power." They followed him because he had amazed them for a long time with his magic. (ACTS 8:9–11)

Briege McKenna is a Catholic nun with an extraordinary healing ministry. She recounts her life story in the book *Miracles Do Happen*. Prior to her ministry, she had a close encounter with a modern-day sorcerer that taught her an essential lesson. At the urging of friends, she consulted a man who others claimed was a "prophet." He seemed to possess extraordinary powers and could tell people things about their lives that only they knew. During the course of her visit with him, she felt increasingly uncomfortable. Even so, she consulted him again. As they talked, she realized the man was trying to destroy her faith and she began to understand the gravity of her mistake: "First, I should not have gone to a 'prophet.' I was trying to see the future. It was like fortune-telling, like seeking a false god. I was doing what God said not to do in the first commandment, 'Thou shalt not put strange gods before me. . . . ' I must leave the future completely to him. Second, I had to learn the difference between judging and discerning. The first time I went to the prophet, I knew something was wrong, but I thought I should not judge him."

As it happened, the Lord delivered Briege from this encounter with magic and, instead, performed a wonderful miracle in her life. It occurred on December 9, 1970. Before that, she had been diagnosed with rheumatoid arthritis so severe that she had to be hospitalized for several months. Briege even wore plaster-of-paris boots for a time in order to prevent her feet from becoming deformed. But nothing really worked. One day she decided to attend a prayer service. Though she brought a laundry list of prayer requests, physical healing wasn't one of them. As she waited for someone to pray with her, she closed her eyes, and felt a hand on her head. But when she looked up, no one was visible. "There was a power going through my body. . . . I felt like a banana being peeled. I looked down. My fingers had been stiff, but not deformed like my feet. There had been sores on my elbows. I looked at myself. My fingers were limber, the sores were gone, and I could see that my feet, in sandals, were no longer deformed. I jumped up screaming, 'Jesus! You're right here!'"

Today, she is a woman of immense energy and joy. Since then, thousands of people have benefited from her ministry, which has taken her to the remote corners of the world.

Imagine what might have happened had Briege listened to that false prophet. She might well be a woman bereft of faith and hope, still crippled by a cruel disease. Instead, she escaped the snares of the enemy to become an emissary of the love of God.

Father, protect me from the deceptions of evil, especially whenever it masquerades as good. Never let my curiosity lead me into places I should not venture. Forgive me for any way I have tried to know more about the future than you would reveal to me. Once again, I commit my life into your hands, trusting that you will give me the grace I need for each day.

A Miracle of Laughter

When [Abraham] was ninety-nine years old, the Lord appeared to him.... Then God said, "Yes, but your wife Sarah will bear you a son, and you will call him Isaac." (GENESIS 17:1, 19)

You may remember the story. Abraham is known as the father of faith, but how did this giant of faith respond to God's promise? Scripture says that he fell down laughing and said to himself, "Will a son be born to a man a hundred years old? Will Sarah bear a child at the age of ninety?" Interestingly, God told him to name his son, "Isaac," which actually means "he laughs." Even God seemed to enjoy the humor of this miracle.

Nearly twenty-five years earlier, God had promised Abraham that he would be father to a great nation. But many years later, he and Sarah were still childless. Both of them must have concluded that God needed help fulfilling his promise. So Sarah suggested that Abraham sleep with her maid, Hagar, in order to have a child. Though this was an accepted practice in ancient cultures, only chaos ensued in their household. Hagar's son, Ishmael, was an affront to Sarah's barrenness. After this, God once again promised to bless Abraham and Sarah with a son.

Why did it take God twenty-five years to perform the miracle he initially promised Abraham? Couldn't he have waved his hand over Sarah, and presto change-o, given her a son? Perhaps God was trying to convey a lesson—that miracles often require the soil of faith and that faith develops through the discipline of waiting. Waiting exposes our weakness, our anxieties, and our need to depend utterly on God. No wonder we dislike it! While action is seen as a sign of strength, waiting indicates that we haven't the power to control our circumstances.

In all honestly, we must admit that sometimes we are looking for magical answers to our prayers. We want a shortcut, instant power to change things in the way we think best. Fortunately, God doesn't give in to us. Instead, he shapes us into men and women of faith by making us endure the agony of waiting. As we get better at it, perhaps God will enable us to enjoy the joke, the divine humor, which delights in turning the wisdom of this world entirely on its head.

> *Lord, help me to remember that your power is made perfect in weakness. Instead of taking pains to show how strong and in control I am, let me join Paul in boasting of my weakness, so that your power may all the more rest on me. As I wait, let my confidence in your promises be so strong that I can actually laugh at the days to come.*

Seven

Miracles of Deliverance

This poor man called, and the Lord heard him;
  he saved him out of all his troubles.
The angel of the Lord encamps around those who fear him,
  and he delivers them.

—PSALM 34: 6–7

It's a wonder I love animals. When I was four years old, I was pinned to the ground by a vicious Great Dane. If my life flashed in front of me then, it was too short to remember the experience. But I will never forget the vision of menacing teeth and angry eyes poised an inch above my nose. Nor will I forget the relief I felt when my older brother rescued me and chased the monster away.

That's how I feel when I think about the way God delivers his people. Scripture warns us to be on guard because our enemy, the devil, prowls around like a roaring lion seeking someone to devour. I don't know about you, but the thought that I could be eaten alive is enough to ruin my day. In fact, I've always been grateful that humans are at the top of the food chain rather than somewhere further down.

But in the spiritual world the unhappy truth is that we are beset by predators. Fortunately, we are protected from such enemies by a power far greater than theirs. As long as we believe in Christ, we need not fear. All that our Deliverer asks is that we cooperate with him through our faith and by living in obedience to him. Knowing this, we can exult with the psalmist:

> Even though I walk
>   through the valley of the shadow of death,
> I will fear no evil,
>   for you are with me;
> your rod and your staff,
>   they comfort me.
> You prepare a table before me
>   in the presence of my enemies.

You anoint my head with oil;
    my cup overflows.
Surely goodness and love will follow me
    all the days of my life,
and I will dwell in the house of the Lord
    forever.

The Miracle of Too Many Frogs

If you refuse to let them [the Israelites] go, I will plague your whole country with frogs. The Nile will teem with frogs. They will come up into your palace and your bedroom and onto your bed, into the houses of your officials and on your people, and into your ovens and kneading troughs. (EXODUS 8:2–3)

For more years than they could remember, the Israelites had been slaves in Egypt. They spoke to one another about the fathers of their race—of Abraham, Isaac, and Jacob, and of Joseph who had once been great in Egypt and who, on his deathbed, had prophesied their deliverance. It was said that these men conversed with God himself. But God was silent now. Silent, that is, until Moses, the Hebrew son of Pharaoh's daughter returned from his exile in the desert, claiming to have talked with God. He spoke of freedom from the tyranny of Egypt and of a promised land where they would dwell in peace and security. And now he and his brother, Aaron, were matching wits with Pharaoh's magicians, attempting to convince the tyrant to let God's people go.

But Pharaoh was stubborn. He refused to listen to Moses and Aaron, even after they changed the River Nile to blood. Now they promised a plague of frogs if Pharaoh would not relent. And he would not. So the frogs came in thousands and covered the land. They were everywhere—in ovens, on beds, underfoot, and even in the bread and water. Then, just as suddenly as they had appeared, the frogs died. From one end of the nation to the other, Egypt reeked of them.

The Israelites must have enjoyed the irony of this plague. They knew that the Egyptians worshiped the frog as a sacred idol, the god of fecundity. Now the God of Israel was rubbing their noses in their idolatry. Where was this mighty god of Egypt when the true God displayed his power?

Scripture tells us that after the frogs died, Pharaoh hardened his heart, refusing to listen to Moses and Aaron. Throughout the Bible, "hardening the heart" involves rejecting God in favor of something else. While obedience softens the heart, sin hardens it. The more the heart disregards its Creator, the less susceptible it will be to grace. With each plague, Pharaoh's heart grew harder and more distant from God.

Clearly, Pharaoh was one of history's bad guys. If we identify with anyone in the story, it's likely to be Moses or the oppressed Israelites. Yet, in common with Pharaoh, we share a heart that is capable of either great good or enormous evil. And like him, we sometimes suffer judgment. We may not wake up with frogs on our pillow, but we will inevitably sample the consequences of our sin. If we drink too much, we will one day find that alcohol has robbed us of our family and our future. If we are disloyal, we may one day face betrayal. If we have judged harshly, we will search in vain for mercy when we need it most. True, we don't always get exactly what we deserve. But sooner or later we usually do get a taste of our own medicine. Bitter though it is, this is the medicine that has the power to deliver us from evil, to heal our hearts and keep them soft.

Father, you tell us that you discipline everyone whom you accept as a son or daughter. When you correct me, help me to realize you are simply treating me as a member of the family. Let me respond in a way that makes my heart as different from Pharaoh's as summer is from winter and as day is from night. Give me grace to admit my sin and ask your forgiveness. As I do, soften my heart and fill it with your presence.

Deliver Me from Evil

Submit yourselves, then, to God. Resist the devil, and he will flee from you. Come near to God and he will come near to you.
(JAMES 4:7–8)

*S*ome things never change. It doesn't matter whether you're talking about ancient Palestine, modern-day America, or somewhere in Asia seventy years ago. The war between good and evil still rages. Sometimes in very dramatic ways.

George Soltau explains that his father lived in South Korea in the early 1920s. T. Stanley Soltau was an itinerant Presbyterian missionary, traveling from one village church to another. He would carry his own food and bedding and spend a short time in each place performing various ministerial duties: examining candidates for baptism, conducting communion services, and preaching.

"Most of his duties were rather routine," explained George. "But there were always surprises. One day he entered a small village only to be greeted by a group of excited men and women. 'Pastor, please come quickly,' they implored. 'We have a woman who is demon-possessed.' When he arrived at the church he saw her. She was raving obscenities, cursing, and writhing uncontrollably. Inexperienced in such matters, he recalled how such incidents were described in the gospels. He quickly organized a prayer team of people who promised to pray around the clock for her. By early evening the exorcism was complete. The demon left and the woman went absolutely limp.

"The next day he made his way over the mountain into the next little valley. As soon as he arrived, the people rushed toward him, telling him that one of the women had become demon-possessed. Just like the other woman, she was ranting and cursing. The villagers had tied her hands so that she couldn't hurt herself or anyone else. Again a prayer team was organized and the woman was set free. When the pastor inquired about the time that she began acting as though she were possessed, he discovered that it was about the same time that the previous woman had been delivered!"

T. Stanley Soltau didn't need to look far for an explanation. He certainly would have recalled the many encounters Jesus had with demonized individuals. He may have even recalled the words of the apostle Peter: "Be self-controlled and alert. Your enemy the devil prowls around like a roaring lion looking for someone to devour. Resist him, standing firm in the faith." He didn't know the two women well enough to know why they had been such easy targets for demonic powers. But he did know that the power of Jesus to deliver them was far stronger than the power of evil to enslave them.

Few of us encounter evil undisguised. Most often it masks itself in subtler disguises. Whatever the case, we needn't fear it as long as we stand firm in faith, calling on the Father to lead us not into temptation and to deliver us from every form of evil.

Lord, I reject Satan and all his works and empty promises. I believe you are God, the Father almighty, creator of heaven and earth. I believe in Jesus Christ, your only Son and my Lord, who died and who rose from the dead. I believe in the Holy Spirit, the resurrection of the body, and life everlasting. Thank you for giving me the grace to believe. Watch over and protect me from every form of evil. And grant that I might live in your presence forever. Amen.

The Miracle of the Boy and the Giant

As the Philistine moved closer to attack him, David ran quickly toward the battle line to meet him. Reaching into his bag and taking out a stone, he slung it and struck the Philistine on the forehead. The stone sank into his forehead, and he fell facedown on the ground. So David triumphed over the Philistine with a sling and a stone; without a sword in his hand he struck down the Philistine and killed him. (1 SAMUEL 17:48–50)

Pitting David against Goliath would have been like sending a glider into battle with a Stealth Bomber. The boy with the slingshot didn't have a chance against a nine-foot colossus, wearing 125 pounds of bronze armor, toting a spear and a sword. But we all know that David got his man despite the odds.

Most of us first heard this story in our childhood. It conjures up proverbs like, "pride cometh before a fall" and "the bigger they are, the harder they fall." And though we may not have thought about it for years, the miracle of David and Goliath is a story that reveals much about our struggle with evil.

You will remember that Goliath had challenged King Saul and the Jews to produce a champion to fight him. If the Jewish champion prevailed, the Philistines would become their subjects. But if Goliath won, the Israelites would become their slaves. For forty days, the giant taunts them, and each day their fear increases as he grows larger and more hideous in their eyes. His threats weave a spell over the Israelites. He is like a spider toying with its prey.

Then David breaks upon the scene and exclaims with youthful indignation, "Who is this uncircumcised Philistine that he should defy the armies of the living God?" Was this courage on the boy's part or stupidity? Knowing the end of the story helps us to tell the difference.

A thousand years later, the story repeats itself, not far from where David fought Goliath. This time the battle takes place in the desert outside Jerusalem and the threatening giant is none other than the devil himself. In the Hebrew Scriptures, the devil is represented by figures like Goliath and Pharaoh, but in the Gospels he comes on the scene undisguised.

Like David, who stripped himself of Saul's protecting armor and sword, Jesus strips himself of bodily strength by fasting. David faced Goliath after forty days of the giant's threats. Now Jesus meets Satan after forty days in the desert. David battled Goliath with a only a stone and a sling, while Jesus defeats Satan with only the word of God.

Over and over the themes echo through Scripture and repeat themselves in the life of faith. God sends deliverance to his people, who are enslaved by sin and Satan. Weakness overcomes strength, humility defeats pride, faith confounds fear, light overcomes darkness. When hope appears to have vanished, victory breaks through. These are the paradoxes upon which faith rests and the life of grace unfolds. As Christ says to Saint Paul and as he says to us today: "My grace is sufficient for you, for my power is made perfect in weakness."

Praise be to the Lord my Rock, who trains my hands for war, my fingers for battle. He is my loving God and my fortress, my stronghold and my deliverer, my shield, in whom I take refuge.

A Miracle in the Night

❧

He reached down from on high and took hold of me; he drew me out of deep waters. He rescued me from my powerful enemy, from my foes, who were too strong for me. They confronted me in the day of my disaster, but the Lord was my support. He brought me out into a spacious place; he rescued me because he delighted in me. (PSALM 18:16–19)

arol Anderson didn't know what to do. Diagnosed with rheumatoid arthritis in 1978, her only escape from excruciating pain was a steady supply of codeine. She couldn't live without it, but her doctor told her she had to try. Otherwise, he couldn't perform the surgery she needed.

Her rheumatologist had been shocked by what he read on her X-rays. Her elbows had been completely eaten away by the disease. He had never seen so much destruction in a patient her age.

Carol knew she was hooked on an opiate, and that she would have to endure the agony of withdrawal. She checked into a local drug-treatment center and was assigned to the detox unit. She tells her story in the November 1991 issue of *Charisma Magazine*:

"I was insulted. They thought I was a junkie and put me on methadone. I looked at my crack-user roommate and piously informed God: 'I don't belong here. I took codeine for the pain.'"

She sensed his answer immediately: "You took drug for the pain in your arms. She took them for the pain in her heart. Don't think yourself better."

The detoxing process was far worse than she feared, complete with chills and night sweats, insomnia, and a sensation like insects crawling all over her body. Finally, one night she felt a presence in her room. "I knew it was the Lord," she explained. "I couldn't see Him with my physical eyes, but I could follow Him as He approached my bedside."

"I sang a song about God and me walking through the field together that I'd learned as a child.... I could feel Him clasp my hand. I could see us walking together."

That night was the beginning of the end of Carol's long nightmare. Her experience reassured her that God was still close by, holding tightly to her hand. After that, she began to hope that he would deliver her from pain and addiction. Shortly afterward, she was released from the treatment center, having kicked her codeine habit. But predictably, the pain returned. One day in church she went forward for prayer. She'd sought prayer so many times it almost seemed pointless. Still some stubbornness inside her refused to stop hoping for a miracle.

Afterward, her pain gradually receded and then disappeared completely. Before long, she found she could use her arms and hands to perform routine tasks like fastening buttons, combing her hair, or opening the clasp of a bracelet.

One day she strode into her surgeon's office, arms to her side, and asked whether he thought surgery was the only hope for restoring her. "He pointed impatiently at the X-rays. 'As I told you before, the damage is irreversible. Your elbows are destroyed. Your only hope is surgery.'

"I let him finish, then bent my arms up and down at the elbows. 'You mean if I don't have surgery, I won't be able to do this?'"

Carol's doctors couldn't explain what had happened to her. But she knew. The God who had taken hold of her hand in the middle of her darkest night, was the one who had done the impossible and delivered her from the power of a terrible disease.

> *Lord, it's easy to believe in your love when the rays of the morning sun take the chill off our bodies and make us glad to be alive. But it's hard to keep faith in the middle of the night when every anxious thought is magnified and every pain is more acutely felt. Still, we know that faith often grows best in the dark. Even so, we ask you to reassure us of your presence when we are most tempted to believe you have abandoned us.*

A Miracle of Light and Dark

Then the Lord said to Moses, "Stretch out your hand toward the sky so that darkness will spread over Egypt—darkness that can be felt." So Moses stretched out his hand toward the sky, and total darkness covered all Egypt for three days. No one could see anyone else or leave his place for three days. Yet all the Israelites had light in the places where they lived. (EXODUS 10:21–23)

Like many people, I am fascinated with caves, though I am not quite sure why. Perhaps some primordial nesting instinct is at work, stirring me to think of them as places of shelter and safety. Though caves can be a refuge, they can also be places of impenetrable darkness, particularly if you are unfortunate enough to be lost deep within one, without flashlight or fire to light the way.

This is how I imagine the Egyptians experiencing the palpable darkness that God sent to them as the ninth of ten plagues. They couldn't even see each other, let alone venture out of their homes for three full days. Worst of all, they had no way of knowing how long the darkness would endure.

Biblical scholars point out that Egypt had what was known as "the *khamsin* period." The *khamsin* was a type of westerly wind that would blow dense masses of fine sand from the desert, intercepting the sun's rays and creating a darkness so thick that it could be felt.

This kind of heavy darkness must have been particularly terrifying in the sun-drenched land of Egypt. It would be as though the sun suddenly slipped out of the California sky. To make matters worse, the darkness dealt a terrible blow to their religious beliefs. The Egyptians actually worshiped the sun god *Ra*. Now the God of the Israelite slaves was mocking their god with the darkness.

The remarkable thing about this plague is that the Israelites escaped the darkness completely. Goshen, the land where they lived, was bathed in sunlight. What a marvelous image of the deliverance God was accomplishing! Egypt itself was enthralled in the darkness of idol worship. Now God would consign them to their darkness. Israel, by contrast, belonged to the God who uttered these words at the creation of the world: "Let there be light." As Genesis tells us, "God saw that the light was good, and he separated the light from the darkness."

Clearly, God was separating his people from the darkness of their bondage in Egypt. With each plague, his power became more apparent. In the end, Pharaoh succumbed to God's cry to "let my people go." And the long night of slavery was ended as the Israelites walked in freedom into the light of God's presence.

Deliver us, Lord, from every form of evil, especially the temptation to put anyone or anything above you. For this is nothing but the worship of idols, which leads only to darkness and death. May we not love children, spouse, security, wealth, freedom, comfort, power, beauty, or position more than we love you. For it is only by living in your presence that we continue to live in the light. You alone are the light of the world, the light that the darkness cannot overcome.

Eight

❧

Miracles of Prophecy

The people who were honored in the Bible were the false prophets. It was the ones we call the prophets who were jailed and driven into the desert, and so on.
—NOAM CHOMSKY

*H*ave you ever taken an aptitude test to discover what sort of career might suit you? Chances are that "prophet" never came up as one of your options. In fact, a prophet is the last thing I would ever want to be. It's just not a cushy job.

Most of the prophets we meet in Scripture paid a terrible price for the role they played. They were ridiculed, run out of town, thrown into pits, beheaded, and otherwise persecuted. Often their stubbornness got them into trouble. They simply refused to stop speaking the truth, no matter how unpalatable it was.

Contrary to popular perception, biblical prophecy did not normally involve foretelling the future. Instead, prophecy was a matter of speaking God's word, often in the midst of a world that despised it. Over the last few thousand years, things really haven't changed. We still ridicule those who expose our foolishness and who tell us that happiness comes from pursuing a life of virtue rather than a life of pleasure. Fortunately, the truth cannot be so easily squelched. It keeps poking its nose into our business, urging us to take it seriously.

Interestingly, the primary role of the biblical prophet was to make God's own people, rather than the surrounding pagan nations, uncomfortable with their sin. And it was the rulers and religious leaders of the day who killed the prophets. Today, we should ask ourselves whether we are plugging our ears to the message of modern-day prophets, men and women who offend our religious prejudices and expose our spiritual pride. If that is the case, we would do well to fall on our faces and ask pardon for our foolishness. For the word of God is "sharper than a two-edged sword" with the power to cut away what is diseased and unhealthy inside our own hearts.

The Miracle of a True Prophet

> *He [Elijah] arranged the wood, cut the bull into pieces and laid it on the wood. Then he said to them, "Fill four large jars with water and pour it on the offering and on the wood." ... The fire of the Lord fell and burned up the sacrifice, the wood, the stones and the soil, and also licked up the water in the trench.* (1 KINGS 18:33, 38)

*N*owadays we are suspicious of people who talk about "the truth," especially when it comes to moral matters or religious faith. Like many people, I dislike the way the truth can be twisted and used as a weapon to control others, especially by religious people. But I have discovered that without real truth, life has no meaning.

Elijah was one of history's most famous prophets, a man who risked his life in the service of truth. It happened one day on Mount Carmel, where Israel had gathered to witness one of the most lopsided contests in biblical history. On one side ranged 450 prophets of the Canaanite god Baal. On the other was the lone figure of Elijah, prophet of the Lord. The object was to lay the carcass of a bull on an altar for sacrifice and then, without benefit of matches, lighter, or magnifying glass to call down fire from heaven. The true god would send fire as a miracle to confirm his power, and either the prophets of Baal or Elijah would be revealed as his true prophets.

The 450 prophets shouted and danced around their sacrifice from morning until evening, but no fire fell from heaven. It must have been a comical scene, for Elijah couldn't help mocking them: "Shout louder. Perhaps your god is asleep, or maybe he's busy or away on a trip." Elijah's taunts spurred them to greater frenzy, but still not even a spark.

Then it was Elijah's turn. He increased the odds against himself to astronomical proportions by pouring water not once, but three times, over his sacrifice. Then he uttered this simple prayer: "O Lord, God of Abraham, Isaac and Israel, let it be known today that you are God in Israel and that I am your servant and have done all these things at your command. Answer me, O Lord, answer me, so these people will know that you, O Lord, are God and that you are turning their hearts back again." He didn't shout or plead, dance, or perform some kind of elaborate ritual. He merely prayed, and the God of all truth sent fire to consume the sacrifice, the wood, the stones, and even the water that had pooled around the altar. The fire that day on Mount Carmel must have given a whole new definition to the word *hot*. By contrast, Baal, the so-called "god of fire," had not produced even one spark to challenge the God of Israel.

The power of one against 450. It was indeed a lopsided contest. For Elijah had an unfair advantage. He had the one who created the universe on his side. He couldn't possibly lose.

Now, like then, truth is often an unpopular choice. The false prophets spoke words that the people welcomed, words of encouragement and comfort. Elijah, on the other hand, spoke of judgment and repentance, words that most of us would find unpleasant and distasteful. In a superficial sense, truth is often not nearly as attractive as falsehood. The latter soothes our consciences and affirms the deceits of our hearts. It turns a blind eye to the worst distortions of our culture, calling the light darkness and the darkness light. It glibly chooses lust over love, convenience over life, and greed over generosity. It enslaves us to our passions and renders us blind and deaf to truth. If we are wise, we will pray for the humility to see and embrace the truth, no matter how unpopular or unpalatable. For in the end, it is only the truth that has the power to set us free.

God, give me the grace to distinguish truth from falsehood, first within my own heart and then in the world around me. Forgive me for the times I have denied or hidden from the truth because I found it too uncomfortable or threatening. Once I know the truth, give me the courage to stand up for it, not as the self-righteous do but as those who humble themselves before its power.

A Miracle of Discernment

Then Saul, who was also called Paul, filled with the Holy Spirit, looked straight at Elymas and said, "You are a child of the devil and an enemy of everything that is right! You are full of all kinds of deceit and trickery.... You are going to be blind, and for a time you will be unable to see the light of the sun." (ACTS 13:9–11)

It was said of Catherine of Siena that she could instantly perceive the true character of anyone she met. Somehow, this fourteenth-century believer knew the secret places in the soul and could measure human beings quite accurately, whether good, bad, or somewhere in-between. I don't know about you, but I doubt I would have been comfortable sitting down for a chat with her.

In this incident, the Apostle Paul seems to have possessed the same gift, at least when it came to diagnosing the character of Elymas, a false prophet and Jewish sorcerer. Paul and Barnabas had just arrived at Paphos in Cyprus and were talking with the proconsul, Sergius Paulus, who was curious to hear the word of God. But Elymas was doing whatever he could to undermine them.

Filled with the Spirit, Paul performs a miracle, first by naming the darkness inside Elymas and then by consigning him to a world of outer darkness. Clearly, the punishment fit the crime. But though there was judgment, there was both grace and mercy in this miracle. For through it, Sergius Paulus was snatched from the power of a false prophet to join the ranks of believers. As for Elymas, his blindness was to be temporary, giving him the opportunity to mend his ways, if he so chose.

Paul's punishment of Elymas may sound harsh. But remember that he himself had been blinded on the road to Damascus some years earlier. He knew firsthand the benefits of a little shock therapy for someone who was lost and leading others astray.

Two thousand years later, the false prophets are still with us. It's the one job description that hasn't changed in centuries. Not long ago, I turned on the television in my hotel room in New York City and discovered I was tuned in to a call-in-show with a twist. By dialing a number you could talk to your very own TV fortune-teller. People were asking the usual questions: Will my love life prosper? Should I stay at my present job or change careers? Will I be able to bear children? Will my husband ever stop cheating on me? The fortune-teller responded with encouraging and definitive answers, even seeming to read the minds of her callers. I felt for the men and women who called in so desperate for guidance. They didn't seem to realize that future-gazing, even if it's a sham, is a deadly game. Nor did they know they were being seduced by half truths and false hopes.

Of course most of today's false prophets operate less blatantly. They may be politicians, celebrities, New Age gurus, or even radio talk-show hosts. Whoever and wherever they are, when they oppose the gospel and promote false religion, they are leading people into darkness.

Wherever shadows dwell, we need discernment. Appearances are often deceiving, but fortunately, we have been given the gift of the Holy Spirit to help us separate the light from the dark.

Lord, I have no interest in looking for a false prophet behind every bush. There's too much name-calling as it is. But you know that I need to be able to tell the difference between the truth and a lie, no matter how attractively the latter is packaged. Help my spirit to stay in tune with yours. If I do come across an Elymas, give me the grace to pray for that person, trusting you to remove the scales from his eyes.

A Tiny Prophecy

From the lips of children and infants you have ordained praise.
(PSALM 8:2)

In May of 1989 Ron and September Aguirre traveled to Florida with their two small children, Ana and Roberto. Four-year-old Ana was especially looking forward to the family vacation, which would take them first to St. Augustine and then on to Orlando for a visit to DisneyWorld. After a short visit, the Aguirre's left St. Augustine on Mother's Day deciding to stop at the old mission on the way out of town. As they wandered the grounds of the mission, they discovered a chapel dedicated to the honor of mothers.

What better way to mark Mother's Day than to pray together as a family in that small chapel, they decided. "Ron and I had been wanting to have another child for some time but weren't able to conceive," explained September. "Though our doctors suggested we take fertility drugs, we didn't feel right about it. So we just kept trying—and praying. That day we asked the kids to pray that Jesus would bless me and that he would give us another baby. We prayed for a few minutes and Ron asked the kids whether they had anything they wanted to say. With a serious look on her little face, Ana said, 'Daddy, I felt like Jesus told me we were going to have a baby and that we should call her Elisabeth.' This startled me since both my mother and I are named

Elisabeth. But I never use my first name and Ana only knew my mother as grandma.

"From there we went on to DisneyWorld and had a great time. But when Ron asked the kids what was most special about the trip, Ana piped up and said that the best part of the vacation was having Jesus tell her that she was going to have a little sister named Elisabeth.

"A month later, I became pregnant. And sure enough, it was a baby girl. Of course we named her Elisabeth. We now have four children and Elisabeth is definitely the feistiest. Our little fireball, she keeps us on our knees asking for the grace to be good parents. I understand that *Elisabeth* actually means grace. Looking back, it's no surprise to me that Elisabeth is the name Jesus whispered to Ana that day in the little chapel in Florida."

Lord, you find so many ways to communicate your love—even through the lips of a small child. Increase our faith and help us to be sensitive to the unexpected ways you sometimes speak. As you answer our prayers, especially for children, give us the grace to respond to those answered prayers in a way that reflects your love.

The Messenger Does Matter

We were met by a slave girl who had a spirit by which she predicted the future. She earned a great deal of money for her owners by fortune-telling. This girl followed Paul and the rest of us, shouting, "These men are servants of the Most High God, who are telling you the way to be saved."... Finally Paul became so troubled that he turned around and said to the spirit, "In the name of Jesus Christ I command you to come out of her!" At that moment the spirit left her. (ACTS 16:16–17, 18)

Paul was in Macedonia when he attracted an annoying groupie. She was a slave girl, possessed by an evil spirit, which apparently gave her the power to predict the future. In fact, her occult powers made a great deal of money for her masters. Interestingly, she repeatedly hails Paul and his companions as servants of the Most High.

Why would an evil spirit speak the truth about Paul's identity and purpose? We don't have a definite answer to this question, but we should remember that one of Satan's most powerful weapons is the truth. Does that shock you? Actually, it would be more accurate to say that truth is one of his favorite weapons as long as it is mixed with a lie. After all, a half-truth is harder to reject than a patent lie. That's why many of his deceptions are so seductive.

Paul may also have realized how dangerous it would be to let an ungodly messenger accompany the preaching of the gospel. It might imply that one could embrace Christianity and occult beliefs at the same time.

The temptation to practice what I call "designer religion" is still with us. We would like to mix and match those elements from various religious faiths that are most attractive to us. Best-selling authors concoct their own designs, to appeal to popular tastes. In the process, of course, they make a good deal of money. Usually, these designer faiths offer an eclectic mixture of conflicting and subjective beliefs, which demand very little from us in terms of commitment, sacrifice, or intellectual honesty. But in the long run, this is the costliest kind of faith because it seduces our souls, distracting us from the claims of the only God who is powerful and loving enough to save us. Of course all truth is God's truth, but ultimately, a "truth" we can control and manipulate is a weak foundation on which to build a life.

By contrast, the gospel that Paul preached was invigorating, life-giving, scandalous, challenging, humbling, costly, and beautiful. To believe it, is to believe it all. To surrender to it, is to give heart and soul to the truth and to be changed forever in the process.

Lord, when it comes to my faith, let me tolerate no half-measures. Take me at my word when I tell you that I long to know you better. And let your word, which is sharper than a two-edged sword, cut away all that is soft and cowardly in me. Help me to pay the price true faith demands. And as I do, may I enjoy all the rewards you promise to those who belong to you.

A Miracle in Battle

The king of Israel brought together the prophets—about four hundred men—and asked them, "Shall I go to war against Ramoth Gilead, or shall I refrain?" "Go," they answered, "for the Lord will give it into the king's hand."

But Jehoshaphat asked, "Is there not a prophet of the Lord here whom we can inquire of?" The king of Israel answered Jehoshaphat, "There is still one man through whom we can inquire of the Lord, but I hate him because he never prophesies anything good about me, but always bad." (1 KINGS 22:6–8)

Try picturing the scene. Ahab was one of Israel's most evil kings. He had forged an alliance with Jehoshaphat, the king of Judah, to wage war against an enemy. Before riding into battle, Ahab consulted four hundred of his prophets and got an answer that was music to his ears: "Ride on to victory. God is on your side."

Only one man challenged the wisdom of the four-hundred. Micaiah stood before Ahab and prophesied his defeat and death in no uncertain terms: "If you ever return safely, the Lord has not spoken through me."

Despite the warning, both kings rode into battle, but not before the crafty Ahab developed a scheme to protect himself. He donned a disguise while the unwitting Jehoshaphat entered the fray still dressed in his royal robes. Ahab knew that a king in royal regalia would prove an easy target for the enemy. In fact the king of Aram had specifically instructed his commanders to search out Ahab and destroy him.

At first Ahab's scheme seemed to work. But then "someone drew his bow at random and hit the king of Israel between the sections of his armor." A foolproof disguise couldn't thwart the fulfillment of the prophecy. The one true prophet made fools out of four hundred liars.

But what can we learn from the story today? Perhaps one lesson is that it doesn't matter how many people say yes when God says no. Too often, we approach the great spiritual and moral questions of our time as though we can find answers by majority vote. But often the majority has its own vested interest in view. It prefers the convenient answer to the inconvenient, the pleasurable to the uncomfortable. It is shaped more by the power of culture than the power of faith.

Most often, true prophets make us uncomfortable. They expose our unfaithfulness, probe our motives, and call us to change. If you really seek wisdom, try to open yourself up to differing points of view, particularly ones that disturb your complacency. Listen especially to the voices of courage in our world today. If you do, you may recognize the "voice that cries in the wilderness," and it may change your life forever.

Father, so often we only tune into those who agree with us. We make friends with people who are like us. We read books by authors who echo our thoughts. We go to church with people who look like us. Lord, shake us out of our familiar comfort zones by the power of your word. Speak to us in whatever way you choose, and give us the courage to listen.

Nine

❧

When Miracles Don't Happen

Men's thirst for the most amazing and indubitable wonders actually stems from a desire for a faith without shadows, for a crown without a cross. . . . A miracle is Christian only if it helps us to believe rather than relieves us of the necessity of faith.
—LOUIS MONDEN, S.J.

I'm a sucker for happy endings. I can enjoy a good novel that is full of tragic moments as long as things turn out reasonably well in the end. But woe to the author who strings me along and then lets me down with a bang. Most often, miracles are stories with tragic elements that have a happy ending. They appeal to our need for wonder and for mercy, for our longing to believe that God does hear our prayers and that he sometimes answers us in supernatural ways. If it were up to us, miracles would be as plentiful as butterflies in summer.

Louis Monden is the author of a fascinating book about miracles entitled *Signs and Wonders*. He offers yet another perspective on our thirst for miracles, pointing out that our desire often stems from an attempt to build a "faith without shadows." Just like the Jews in ancient Palestine, we clamor for "a sign from heaven." And like the Apostle Thomas, we will believe only if we can touch and see the wounds of the risen Christ ourselves. But as Monden says, miracles merely help us "to believe rather than relieve us of the necessity of faith."

Despite our longings, we do not live in a perfect world. The promise of heaven is not yet fulfilled. As Monden points out, miracles "should not give the impression that this passing world is now already glorified, that Paradise has already been regained. The miracle must rather give a glimpse of what is to come; it is a kind of smile by which God lightens the path of his Church...." What a wonderful image—a smile that lightens our path.

Scripture talks about life as a "valley of tears," and so it often is. But it is in the midst of tears and darkness that the deepest faith develops. Wherever and whenever miracles don't happen, we have an opportunity to allow faith to take root in our souls, and it is precisely this faith that has the power to work the deepest miracle of all, the one that happens quietly inside our own hearts.

If you have been asking for a miracle with no results, remember that God still loves you and hasn't forgotten you. Nor is he indifferent to your suffering. Don't let your faith depend on miracles, but instead, ask God to accomplish his purposes even if he doesn't answer your prayers in precisely the way you hope he will.

A Faith without Miracles

Now Thomas (called Didymus), one of the Twelve, was not with the
disciples when Jesus came. So the other disciples told him, "We have
seen the Lord!" But he said to them, "Unless I see the nail marks in his
hands and put my finger where the nails were, and put my hand into
his side, I will not believe it." (JOHN 20:24–25)

Somehow, Thomas's skepticism comforts me. It reminds me that
I'm not the only doubter in the kingdom of God, the only one
who sometimes feels abandoned and confused.

It must have been easy enough for Thomas to believe when he
could sit across the table from Jesus, sharing the same loaf of bread and
drinking from the same cup, or when he could see the sick healed and
the dead raised. Even though the disciples of Jesus had no money and
no place to lay their heads at night, the work was exhilarating. Word of
Jesus' miracles had spread throughout Israel. Each day, more followers
were added to their number. Soon they would be a force no power on
earth could resist. And Thomas would be there to see Israel restored,
with a great king sitting on the throne. It was wonderful to have a
vision, for he knew that without a vision the people would perish.

But Thomas's faith was shattered at Calvary. His hopes were laid
in the grave along with the body of Jesus. He must have felt a terrible
sense of grief, confusion, and loss. So much so that he seems to have
responded angrily when the other disciples claimed to have seen the

risen Jesus. "No, I refuse to believe you. Unless I see the nail marks with my own eyes and feel the wounds with my fingers, I will not believe."

It's easy to criticize Thomas for his unbelief. But if you have ever given heart and soul to some cause or some person only to be disappointed, you will understand his anger.

Sometimes our disappointment and disillusionment centers on the church itself. We may have been part of a church that has fallen apart, destroyed by scandal or internal rivalries. We may have given the better part of our youth to some cause that has since been discredited or become distorted. Or perhaps we feel that God has abandoned us when we needed him most. A spouse has left, a child has died, a friend has turned her back on us. We have prayed for faith, for healing, for grace, but have been met with silence. We have asked for a cup of water and been given vinegar instead. When this happens, youthful idealism is in danger of evolving into cynicism. We don't want to believe again, to be tricked and fooled and disappointed. So we become angry in order to protect ourselves.

But our disappointment needn't make us allergic to faith. Thomas was disappointed because he did not understand Jesus and the real work he had come to do. Because he could not see why Jesus had to die, he could not at first believe in his resurrection. Like Thomas's, our immature faith is not so much faith in Jesus as in a poster-like image of him that we have painted—someone who always acts lovingly as we define love; who answers our prayers, especially when they are reasonable; and who never does anything we can't understand. But the real Jesus refuses to let us settle for a false portrait of himself. One after the other, he keeps erasing our distorted pictures. It isn't as though Jesus has discarded love, faithfulness, and compassion from his palette. It's just that he adds deeper hues to them, so that eventually we will gaze upon a Rembrandt rather than the stick-figure drawing we started with.

As our false images are shattered, we may see only darkness for a time. What used to comfort, will comfort us no longer. We may even feel deeply disillusioned. But being disillusioned is a good thing if it means an illusory spell has been broken. If we cling to God during this time, our faith will return to us as a ripened fruit. We will enjoy deeper intimacy with Jesus and greater freedom and peace in our personal lives. The darkness will give way to light and we will know even as we are known.

Lord, just when I think I have you figured out, you upset everything. When will I learn that only the pure in heart will see you face to face? I am beginning to realize that your work of purification happens best in darkness, when you seem distant though you are near. Help me to have courage as I let go of what is false in order to reach into the darkness to take hold of what is true.

Turning Stones to Bread

After fasting forty days and forty nights, he [Jesus] was hungry. The tempter came to him and said, "If you are the Son of God, tell these stones to become bread." (MATTHEW 4:2–3)

After forty days in the wilderness, it would have been easy for Jesus to picture stones turning to bread. What starving man wouldn't? Like bread, the smooth, round stones fit snugly into the palm of his hand. He could almost smell the loaves baking in the desert heat. He had only to speak a word to perform this small miracle. But he didn't. Instead, he reminded the devil, "Man does not live on bread alone, but on every word that comes from the mouth of God."

Later, Jesus would tell the crowds, "I am the bread of life. He who comes to me shall never be hungry." And again he would speak of bread: "Which of you, if his son asks for bread, will give him a stone? If you know how to give good things to your children, how much more will your Father in heaven give good things to those who ask him."

Yet despite our faith, sometimes we are hungry. And sometimes we are tempted to believe that God has handed us a stone when we asked for bread. We plead for the bread of financial blessing, and we go bankrupt. We ask for the bread of a loving spouse, and we remain single. We beg for the bread of success, and we fail. Where is this bread that Jesus speaks of that we are so hungry for? If we had the power to turn our stones to bread, we would do so in an instant.

Yet sometimes we do have that power. We can cheat to obtain the money we want. We can sleep around to get the love we need. We can play games and dirty tricks to get ahead. And for a while, this bread will feed us. But it will never satisfy.

Jesus wasn't exaggerating when he called himself the bread of life. He's the one who nourishes our souls. If you have tried but failed to satisfy your cravings, bring them to Jesus once again. Spend some time quietly in his presence. Tell him what you are feeling, and ask him to show you the truth of his word and of his promise. It may be that your hunger will lead you to a deeper experience of his sufficiency.

Lord, you have created us with spiritual hungers, cravings that are not easily satisfied. Help me to resist the temptation to stuff myself with cheap substitutes, and, instead, help me to pursue you as the source of my life. When I am tempted to turn stones to bread through my own power, give me courage to trust your word so that it will nourish my soul.

A Temporary Miracle

The eternal God is your refuge, and underneath are the everlasting arms. (DEUTERONOMY 33:27)

an and Dale Goorhouse were more than brothers. They were identical twins and best friends who roomed together in college. After they married, they lived just two blocks apart. As far as they knew, they would spend the rest of their lives, working hard, raising their children, and one day recognizing their own age-worn features in each other's faces. But suddenly that familiar and comforting vision of the future vanished. Without warning, Dale was diagnosed with lung cancer.

"It was such a shock," Dan explained. "Dale was an athlete. Someone who ate right and who took care of himself. He never even smoked. We just couldn't believe he had lung cancer. He and I were products of the same environment. We shared the same genetic make-up. How could he possibly be sick when I was perfectly healthy? I couldn't stop asking the question.

"His doctors prescribed the most aggressive course of chemotherapy they could. After he completed it, they performed a CAT scan, which revealed spots on his liver, one kidney, and his spine. Dale's oncologist was almost certain the cancer had spread. If it had, surgery to remove the cancerous lung would be pointless. If not, it might save his other lung and his life.

"Neither Dale nor I were very religious at that time. We had been brought up in the Mormon church but had left it in our late teens. Since then, we had attended a couple of different Christian churches, but we weren't too serious about it. They say that in foxholes even atheists believe in God. I guess cancer was that foxhole for Dale and me. Both of us began to pray for a miracle along with our entire family. None of us were ready for Dale to die.

"It happened when Dale was alone, lying on a gurney, waiting to go in for another set of X-rays. He was praying that God would heal his kidney and liver, erasing the spots so that the doctors would have enough confidence to remove the cancerous lung. He asked God to give him a sign that he heard his prayers, and then something very strange happened. Dale told me that he felt his body being lifted off the gurney. For a few moments, he was simply suspended in the air. There was no rational explanation for what happened to him. Even so, he wasn't the least bit afraid. Instead, he said he felt an incredible sense of peace. He knew then that the doctors wouldn't find those spots. He was so sure, he even told the X-ray technician that nothing would show up on the film.

"And Dale was right. The oncologist was extremely surprised when he reviewed the X-rays and found no evidence of cancer. The whole family felt that God had done something wonderful for Dale. It was the beginning of real faith for us all.

"The doctors performed the surgery, and Dale just got stronger and stronger. For five months he felt great. His hair grew back, and he looked the picture of health. But then, almost two years after the initial diagnosis, the doctors found cancer in the other lung. Though I became physically ill when Dale told me the news, he assured me that he was at peace about it—and I knew he was. He encouraged me to stop worrying because everything was in God's hands.

"We learned of the cancer's recurrence in January. Dale died on February twenty-fifth. Looking back on it, I'm not sure why God healed him only temporarily. But I do know that my family and I will never be the same because of what happened. It gave us time to deal with his death, and it made us closer as a family. Our faith is so much stronger now.

"Somehow, I drew strength from the way Dale handled himself. I'm very proud of how much courage and trust he showed. Now I try to teach my own boys to love and appreciate each other, realizing that life is such a fragile thing."

Dan and his family are grateful for the miracle that Dale experienced even if it simply delayed his death by a few months. Somehow, it must have convinced Dale that God was real and that he was in charge of everything that happened. Through the days that preceded his death, he may well have felt the strong arms of God still holding him, just like that day he was raised up on the gurney.

He may even have realized that every healing is really only temporary. Each of us will one day die. We will certainly lose the people we love the most. But such miracles help convince us that God is near, tenderly carrying us in his arms, watching over us as we let go of this life to take hold of the next.

Father, you are our refuge in time of trouble. No one can comfort us like you do. No one has arms powerful and tender enough to hold us when we are sick and hurting. Help us to remember that these are the very same arms that will one day raise us from our graves to enjoy everlasting life in your presence.

A Better Way Than Miracles

An angel of the Lord appeared to Joseph in a dream. "Get up," he said, "take the child and his mother and escape to Egypt. Stay there until I tell you, for Herod is going to search for the child to kill him." . . . When Herod realized he had been outwitted . . . he was furious, and he gave orders to kill all the boys in Bethlehem and its vicinity who were two years old and under. (MATTHEW 2:13, 16)

An angel warned Joseph to flee Bethlehem from the wrath of a wicked king. And Joseph heeded the warning. Through a miracle, God saved his infant Son. Yet many baby boys were slaughtered in Jesus' stead. Why was there no miracle for them? Why does there seem to be no miracle for so many innocent children today?

Recently, I watched a television documentary that broke my heart. It was an exposé of the consequences of China's "one-child policy." Because of overpopulation, the Chinese government has made it unlawful for a family to have more than one child. Because Chinese culture values males more than females, millions of baby girls have been aborted or abandoned. Those that have been abandoned often die in orphanages, where conditions are unspeakable.

Such stories force us to confront the most difficult question in the world. Why does God allow evil? Why does he perform miracles for a few of us, while the many suffer? Easy answers elude us.

In Herod's case, God chose not to contravene the will of a wicked ruler. In fact, this seems to be his preferred style of relating to human beings, both good and evil. He allows us the freedom of choice, though, eventually, we are judged as to how well or poorly we use that freedom. Inevitably, our misuse of it has the power to destroy others.

Sometimes, though, evil is rampant because good people stand by and do nothing. Unlike us, God realizes that supernatural acts of power are not always the most effective method for diminishing evil. Instead, he tells us to overcome evil with good. He prefers to unleash the power of his love through ordinary men and women, who decide to shelter the homeless, adopt a child, or find ways to bring solace to the afflicted.

Whatever God is asking, try to be generous. Who knows whether he may want to mold you into a living miracle, a flesh-and-blood answer to someone else's prayer?

Father, I pray that the grief I feel when confronted by tragedy will be harnessed for your purposes. Rather than feeling oppressed by evil, let me seek to be an instrument in your hand. Unite me with others, so that together our love might be a light that overcomes the darkness.

The Dangers of the Gospel

*On Herod's birthday the daughter of Herodias danced for them and pleased Herod so much that he promised with an oath to give her whatever she asked. Prompted by her mother, she said, "Give me here on a platter the head of John the Baptist." (*MATTHEW 14:6–8)

Jesus called his cousin John the greatest man who ever lived. Yet John languished in prison and was cruelly murdered in the midst of Herod's birthday celebration. His head on a platter must have made for a macabre ending to that particular party.

What had John done to deserve this fate? He had spoken the simple truth, declaring that Herod and Herodias were unlawfully married because she had already been wed to Philip, Herod's brother. By so doing, John made a deadly enemy.

After John's death, the disciples must have recalled Jesus' words: "Anyone who does not take his cross and follow me is not worthy of me. Whoever finds his life will lose it, and whoever loses his life for my sake will find it." John had not shirked his cross. He had spoken the truth and paid the ultimate price.

Were the disciples shocked by what happened to John? Did they have second thoughts about following Jesus? Certainly they must have realized the dangerous climate in which their Master moved. Perhaps for the first time, they realized that he really meant what he said: "Do not suppose that I have come to bring peace to the earth. I did not come to bring peace, but a sword." "All men will hate you because of me, but he who stands firm to the end will be saved."

This is not the kind of message that most of us easily embrace. Instead we do our best to tame it by reducing the hard sayings of Jesus to the softness of metaphors. Rather than a tortured body hanging on a bloody cross, we see only the lovely gold crosses we wear around our necks. Or we limit the potency of his message by confining it to its historical context. Of course people suffered. But that was two thousand years ago, when Christianity was just getting established.

But the gospel is as dangerous today as it was when Jesus first preached it. It is an affront to evil that will be met with determined resistance, both within our hearts and in the world at large. Though we haven't the power to remove all the external barriers, we can ask God to demolish the obstacles within our souls. As we do, we will find that the presence of Jesus will grow strong within us, enabling us to do whatever he asks.

Lord, the effect of your word is like a bucket of cold water thrown on a sleeping man. Wake me with the bracing freshness of the truth. Rather than bending your word to make it fit me better, I ask that you would conform me to its power.

Ten

Miracles and Dreams

How much there is in the Bible about dreams. There are, I think, some sixteen chapters in the Old Testament and four or five in the New in which dreams are mentioned, and there are many other passages scattered throughout the book which refer to visions. If we believe the Bible, we must accept the fact that, in the old days, God and his angels came to men in their sleep and made themselves known in dreams.
—ABRAHAM LINCOLN

*M*ore often than not, we ignore our dreams. The more colorful of these sometimes merit a morning's retelling, but after that we forget them. Bad dreams are chalked up to the exotic meal we consumed the night before or to a nagging anxiety that crept into our brain in the middle of the night. But that's about all the stock many of us place in our dreams.

But what if there's more to them than meets the eye? Can God ever speak to us through our dreams? A quick review of Scripture indicates that God spoke powerfully through dreams. A few of the biblical characters whose lives were affected by dreams included Abraham, Jacob, Joseph, Samuel, Saul, Solomon, Joseph (the father of Jesus), and the Apostle Peter. In fact, the early Christian church believed that God sometimes revealed his will through dreams.

Though dreams are often complex and difficult to understand, I believe they may convey spiritual messages to those willing to listen. Of course there is danger in paying too much attention to our dreams. We can become overly introspective and unbalanced if we become obsessed with them, forgetting that dreams are just one avenue, and not the main one, by which God visits us.

In truth, our Creator can use whatever means he chooses to communicate with us. Perhaps he sometimes touches us while we sleep, because he knows we are more vulnerable then. A vivid dream may penetrate our defenses in a way that other methods of communication would not. At the very least, the stories that follow encourage us to be open to the variety of ways God works in our lives.

If you have been ignoring your dreams, it may be time to pay closer attention. As you do, remember to put your dreams into the context of what God has already revealed in his Word. And never make a big decision based only on a dream. Otherwise, you may mistake other voices for the voice of God.

A Dream of Amazing Grace

Then he showed me Joshua the high priest standing before the angel of the Lord, and Satan standing at his right side to accuse him. The Lord said to Satan, "The Lord rebuke you, Satan! The Lord, who has chosen Jerusalem, rebuke you! Is not this man a burning stick snatched from the fire?" (ZECHARIAH 3:1–2)

John Newton is famous for having penned the well-known hymn "Amazing Grace." Before his conversion, however, he lived an anything-but-Christian life as a seaman and slave trader. In his autobiography, he tells the story of a vivid dream he had, some twenty years before he entered the ministry.

Newton dreamed he was standing on the deck of his ship one night, in the harbor of Venice, when suddenly a man approached and showed him a ring. The man gave the ring to the sailor, stressing that it would bring him much happiness and success. He also warned him that if he ever lost the ring, he would know only trouble and misery. Newton accepted the ring gladly, assuring the man he would keep it safe.

As soon as the first man departed, a second man took his place. He wasted no time but began to inquire about the ring. Newton repeated what he had been told about its value, but this man seemed surprised that anyone would ever be foolish enough to place such importance on a mere ring. Before long, he was urging the sailor to toss it overboard. In the dream, Newton did just that, saying: "At last I plucked it off my finger and dropped it over the ship's side into the water; which it had no sooner touched, than I saw, the same instant, a terrible fire burst out from a range of the mountains, (a part of the Alps), which appeared at some distance behind the city of Venice. I saw the hills ... and they were all in flames. I perceived, too late, my folly; and my tempter with an air of insult, informed me, that all the mercy God had in reserve for me was comprised in that ring which I had willfully thrown away. I understood that I must now go with him to the burning mountains.... I trembled, and was in a great agony."

The dream continued and Newton met another man, who asked him why he was so sad. He explained that he had ruined himself and deserved no pity. Then the man asked him whether he would be wiser the second time around if the ring were returned to him. Before Newton could respond, the stranger threw himself over the side of the boat and plunged beneath the surface of the water where the ring had been dropped. Then he surfaced with the ring in hand and climbed back aboard the ship. Immediately, the flames of the mountains were extinguished.

The dream troubled Newton for two or three days, so much so that he could hardly eat or sleep. But eventually he forgot about it. He would not think of it again for several years, when as he says, "I found myself in circumstances very nearly resembling those suggested by this extraordinary dream, when I stood helpless and hopeless upon the brink of an awful eternity."

Fortunately, John Newton became one of history's great converts and went on to write hymns that have inspired believers throughout the world. Like a brand plucked from the fire, he was eventually saved by the mercy of a loving God.

Amazing grace, how sweet the sound, that saved a wretch like me! I once was lost, but now am found, was blind but now I see. Through many dangers, toils, and snares, I have already come; 'tis grace has brought me safe thus far, and grace will lead me home.

A Dream of Glory

Joseph had a dream, and when he told it to his brothers, they hated him all the more. He said to them, "Listen to this dream I had: We were binding sheaves of grain out in the field when suddenly my sheaf rose and stood upright, while your sheaves gathered around mine and bowed down to it." (GENESIS 37:5–7)

At seventeen, Joseph was the favorite son of the patriarch Jacob and the least favorite brother of his ten half-brothers. Perhaps it was youthful naïveté that led him to share a dream that would only pour fuel on the fire of their hatred.

Before long, his glorious dream had given birth to a living nightmare. Still chafing from the insult, the brothers spotted him one day in the field and said to each other, "Here comes that dreamer. Let's get rid of him once and for all. Then we'll see what comes of his dreams." Instead of murdering him, they decided to sell him, for eight ounces of silver, to some Midianite traders en route to Egypt. The once-favored son had become a slave in a foreign country. His dream, it seemed, was nothing more than a childish fantasy.

But in fact, the dream was unfolding even in the midst of Joseph's enslavement and imprisonment. Circumstances eventually brought him to the attention of Pharaoh himself, who gave him great powers over his kingdom. Before long, Joseph's brothers came begging for bread in the midst of a severe famine. When they did, Scripture says, "they bowed down to him with their faces to the ground." After years of trial and hardship, the dream was finally fulfilled and Joseph was able to provide refuge for his father and his brothers in a season of famine.

The seventeen-year-old Joseph couldn't have known that his dream was only part of the picture—the happy ending to a story that would have more than its share of tragic twists and turns. Though Joseph lived thousands of years ago, his experience is still fresh for those who understand it.

Like Joseph, we have been given grace to know the conclusion of the story—the happy ending that awaits those who love God. Still, God doesn't reveal everything that will happen to us along the way. We are yet living between the dream and its fulfillment. We know that Christ has conquered all our enemies, even death, and yet we experience many small deaths each day. We still sin, we still hurt one another, we still suffer from unfulfilled longings. When we are tempted to think that faith is nothing but a childish fantasy, let us remember Joseph's story and take heart. He didn't abandon the dream and neither can we.

Father, you work in mysterious ways, often in ways that confound human wisdom. The more I know of you, the more I realize there is to know. Help me to remember that you give us dreams at night, in the midst of darkness. Let those dreams strengthen me, especially when I am living through a particularly dark time in my life. Let me hold on to the dream and live it out in the power of your Spirit.

A Warrior's Dream

"Not by might nor by power, but by my Spirit," says the Lord Almighty. (ZECHARIAH 4:6)

Francis Bernardone was the son of one of Assisi's most successful merchants. Like the heroes he admired in the legends of King Arthur, he knew he was destined for a life of chivalry and glory. Deciding to enlist on the side of Pope Innocent III in the battle that raged after the death of the Emperor Henry VI, Francis joined a troop from Assisi and set out for Apulia, where they would join the army of Duke Walter III of Brienne. Afire with youthful zeal, it is hardly surprising that he dreamed of war and weapons on his way to battle.

In his dream, Francis stood in his father, Pietro's, shop. He thought perhaps he was there to say farewell. But instead of rolls of beautiful cloth filling the shelves, he saw only a magnificent array of shields, spears, and armor. Then he heard a voice say, "All this shall belong to you and your warriors."

He awoke with new zeal and an urgency to reach the battle lines. But he never made it to Apulia. Instead, he became ill with a fever. Suddenly, as he lay in bed in Spoleto, between sleep and waking, he heard a voice asking where he wanted to go.

"To Apulia to be a knight," he answered.

"Tell me, Francis, who can benefit you most: the Lord or the servant?"

"The Lord," replied Francis.

"Then why do you desert the Lord for the servant and the Prince for his vassal?" the voice challenged.

Francis cried out: "Lord, what do you wish me to do."

The reply came: "Go back to your home. There it shall be told you what you are to do. For the vision you saw must be understood in another way!" Francis awoke and returned home the next day.

The voice and the dream changed the course of Francis' life. No longer roused by visions of earthly glory, he found his old life of cheerful extravagance increasingly distasteful. Before long, his passion for earthly kingdoms was transferred to a kingdom not of this world. In the end, he became one of Christianity's most endearing and remarkable saints. Thousands were to follow his footsteps, living a life of poverty and prayer, preaching the gospel wherever they went and renewing the church by their example. They were spiritual soldiers in the army of a great Prince. Like Francis, they had clothed themselves in the full armor of God, the shining armor he had seen in his dream so many years ago.

Father, zeal without wisdom leads only to ruin. Help us to remember that we need to put on the full armor of the Spirit before venturing out in your service: the belt of truth, the breastplate of righteousness, the gospel of peace, the shield of faith, the helmet of salvation, and the sword of the Spirit, which is the word of God. Then, armed and ready, let us serve you, like Francis, with all the passion our hearts can muster.

"I Dreamed I Won the Lottery"

Therefore I tell you, do not worry about your life, what you will eat or drink; or about your body, what you will wear.... Look at the birds of the air; they do not sow or reap or store away in barns, and yet your heavenly Father feeds them. Are you not much more valuable than they? (MATTHEW 6:25)

Who hasn't dreamed of or at least joked about winning the lottery? Patti Matthews was a college student strapped for cash. An occasional pizza was a stretch for her pocketbook, so it's no surprise that one night she dreamed she hit it big. She watched transfixed as the white balls percolated in the lottery cage. Then one by one, the chosen few came to rest side by side, numbers up. These weren't just any numbers either. They were identical to those printed on the ticket she clutched in her hand. She had won! Before she knew it, someone was pressing a huge wad of money into her hands.

"I was so excited," she said. I began counting it and thinking of all the wonderful things I would buy—a boat, a car, a house. I kept thinking of new things and kept counting my money. But as I did, I noticed that something was happening to the face on the bills. Instead of the face of one of the Presidents, the face on the bill became contorted and evil-looking. It frightened me so much that I threw the money down, not wanting anything to do with it, and woke up.

"As I thought about the dream, I realized that my response to the windfall had been entirely selfish. It hadn't even occurred to me to give some of the money to someone in need. I only wanted it for myself. It got me thinking about how I used money, even though I didn't have much at the time. I knew that the money itself wasn't the problem, it was my attitude toward it. The dream affected me so much that I put a twenty-dollar bill in the collection plate that Sunday—a fortune to me at the time. It was my way of telling God that I trusted him to provide and that I wanted to be generous with whatever he gave me."

Our daydreams about winning the lottery are probably harmless enough. But I wonder what they reveal. In my case, striking it rich appeals to me not so much because of all the neat things I could buy, but because it represents a certain kind of security, and when I think of security I think of Brink's trucks, Swiss bank accounts, or Fort Knox—places to store money and keep it safe. But God doesn't seem to think that way. Instead of storehouses, he speaks of fountains and springs, manna and daily bread given from the Father's hand. In each case, we receive what we need for the moment. We must rely on God to keep the spring alive, the fountain flowing. In such circumstances, it requires faith to be generous with what we have.

Of course I don't believe there is anything wrong with saving money for the future. Wise people do. But there is something wrong if we hoard our money, thinking it will save us from future calamity. Money or no money, lotto or no lotto, our trust is in the Lord, who made heaven and earth. He alone can save us and keep us secure.

Father, I admit that I don't like to depend on you for everything. Sometimes, I would like a little backup, in case you don't come through the way I think you should. Forgive me for my selfishness and lack of trust and enlarge my heart so that I may be as generous to others as you have been to me. Let me see money, not as a tool to keep fear at bay but as an instrument for your glory.

An Enemy's Dream

Gideon arrived just as a man was telling a friend his dream. "I had a dream," he was saying. "A round loaf of barley bread came tumbling into the Midianite camp. It struck the tent with such force that the tent overturned and collapsed." His friend responded, "This can be nothing other than the sword of Gideon son of Joash, the Israelite. God has given the Midianites and the whole camp into his hands."
(JUDGES 7:13–14)

I'll never forget a scene from my childhood. One day, as I was walking down the dirt road that led to our home, I was startled by a spectacle that looked like something out of a Saturday morning cartoon. Two creatures were tearing across a lawn, one in hot pursuit of the other. It wasn't the classic case of dog chasing cat, or even cat chasing dog. Instead, a tiny little chipmunk was furiously pursuing our neighbor's hefty black dog. I'm not certain whether the dog or the chipmunk was more deranged. But I couldn't help laughing at the sight.

Somehow, Gideon and the Midianites remind me of that ferocious chipmunk and cowardly dog. Gideon was the leader of the Israelites, at war with Midian. Before attacking the Midianite camp, God told him to trim his troops. He didn't want Gideon and his sizable army to take credit for the coming victory. It wasn't just a case of

God asking him to tie one arm behind his back. Before he was through, Gideon had excused 31,700 men from a total force of 32,000. He was left with less than one percent of his army to fight an enemy that was too numerous to count.

Still, God assured him of victory and invited Gideon to eavesdrop on the enemy before attacking. That's when Gideon overheard the man's dream. As soon as he heard it, he worshiped God and returned to his camp to rally the troops. Together, 300 men found a way to trick the Midianites into thinking they were an enormous army. As soon as the Israelites blew their trumpets, their enemies awoke to pandemonium. Filled with terror and divinely inspired confusion, they turned on each other with their swords and then fled.

That day God did what only God can do: he used the weak and powerless to rout the strong and mighty. He used 300 men to defeat an army of many thousands.

I must admit that the tactics of God sometimes make me extremely uncomfortable. In fact, he often asks us to do things in a way that contradicts our most basic instincts. Jesus himself excelled at this: "If someone strikes you on the right cheek, turn the other cheek," "If someone forces you to go one mile, go with him two miles," "love your enemies and pray for those who persecute you," "anyone who seeks to save his own life, will lose it." God's ways scandalize us because they contradict the basic values of our fallen world, the only world we have ever really known. Without the gifts of grace and faith, we could not possibly respond as he desires. But with them, we can learn to trust in a God who never fails and never forsakes us, a God whose word is true and whose wisdom is deeper than anything we can comprehend.

Father, you know that Gideon didn't start out as a man of faith, but that he became one because of your faithfulness. Help me to remember how faithful you have been in my own life so that I may be quick to trust you, quick to say yes, despite my fears.

Eleven

❧

Miracles and Visions

From my infancy until now, in the seventieth year of my age, my soul has always beheld this Light. . . . The brightness which I see is not limited by space and is more brilliant than the radiance around the Sun. . . . Sometimes when I see it, all sadness and pain is lifted from me, and I seem a simple girl again, and an old woman no more.
—HILDEGARD OF BINGEN

I confess that the only kind of vision I've ever had happened after twenty-four hours on the road. Actually, it was more like a waking dream, where fantasy blended with reality as I hovered on the brink of sleep. Fortunately, I wasn't the one behind the wheel. My job was merely to help keep the driver awake.

But real visions have little in common with hallucinations, however induced. Rather than distorting our perception of the natural world, authentic spiritual visions remove the barrier between the natural and the supernatural. For a moment in time, they offer a glimpse of a supernatural reality, which was hitherto hidden from us.

Spiritual visions may be the rarest of miracles. But when they happen, they may change the course of history, give us the courage to spread the gospel, or paint a vision of paradise to sustain us. Even so, we shouldn't be overly credible when someone claims to have had such a vision. Nor should we rule out the possibility entirely. Whatever the case, we should remember that true visions come unbidden. They are never something we control.

Ultimately, the only vision we should really desire is the one that will satisfy our longings and put an end to all our suffering. Scripture says that this vision is obtained only by the pure of heart, for they are the ones who will see God. As those who love him, our true destiny is to one day gaze into the face of the God of the Universe and live to tell about it. In fact, that's what Paradise is all about.

The Vision of a Conquering Cross

The Lord is my rock, my fortress and my deliverer; my God is my rock, in whom I take refuge, my shield and the horn of my salvation. He is my stronghold, my refuge and my savior—from violent men you save me. I call to the Lord, who is worthy of praise, and I am saved from my enemies. (2 SAMUEL 22:2–4)

For the first three hundred years of its life, Christianity grew despite tremendous persecution, first in Israel and then throughout the Roman Empire. But early in the fourth century, a man named Constantine had a vision that changed everything.

Constantine was an unlikely contender for the throne of the Roman Empire. Passed over for the rank of Caesar, he fled to Britain, where he joined his father's army. After a while, his position improved and he decided to move against Rome. However, before challenging Maxentius at the Milvian Bridge, he decided to seek God, asking him to reveal himself and pleading for his help. As he was praying during the middle of the day, he saw a cross of light appear in the heavens, above the sun, bearing the inscription, *Conquer by This*. The cross was in the form of the letter X with a perpendicular line drawn through it and turned round at the top like the letter P.

He spent hours wondering what the vision might mean and finally fell asleep perplexed. In the ensuing dream, Christ appeared to him with the identical sign that had been emblazoned in the sky and commanded him to use this cross as a safeguard in every battle. So

Constantine placed it on the shields of all his soldiers. Thus armed, they won the victory, and this cross became the insignia of every Christian emperor since Constantine. Shortly after the battle, the new emperor issued the Edict of Milan which eventually wiped out persecution throughout the Roman Empire.

Author Morton Kelsey links the story of Constantine to a famous twentieth-century military leader: General George Patton. Though Patton did not claim to see a cross in the sky, he awoke from sleep in 1944 with an inspiration that helped determine the outcome of the Battle of the Bulge. Patton summoned Joe Rosevich, his personal secretary, to his office at 4:00 A.M. one December morning. Still in his pajamas, Patton began dictating, laying out a strategy for an attack to begin at precisely the time the Germans would mount their attack. Rosevich later reported that as a result of Patton's strategy, the Nazis "were stopped cold in their frozen tracks." A few days later, Patton told Rosevich that he had suddenly awakened that night at 3:00 A.M. for no apparent reason. When he went to bed, he had no idea the German attack was coming. But when he woke, he was certain it was imminent, and he also knew exactly how to counter it. Patton didn't claim divine inspiration for his insight. But whether it was intuition working at some deep level or the result of a divinely inspired dream, something marvelous had occurred that changed the course of the battle.

> *Lord, often you work in strange and unexpected ways. Help us to hear and recognize your voice no matter how it comes to us, through Scripture, the encouragement of friends, the counsel of the wise—even in dreams and visions. And when we recognize it as your voice, let us be quick to respond.*

A Vision in the Clouds

I looked, and there before me was a white horse! Its rider held a bow, and he was given a crown, and he rode out as a conqueror bent on conquest. (REVELATION 6:2)

*S*anta Rosa is a sleepy little village in Brazil. Without electricity, sidewalks, or even a corner grocery store, it has little to attract the outsider. Still, one man felt drawn to this village, where the Arapiun Indians make their home. It was 1992 and his name was Raimundinho (Little Raymond), an itinerant evangelist who lived on a boat and preached the gospel up and down the river. Before long, his words would transform this languid backwater village into a nest of angry hornets.

It began while Raimundinho was still on his way to Santa Rosa. Approaching a nearby village, he saw a vision in the clouds—a large church building with a tiny door. As he stared, the door of the church began to enlarge until it spanned the entire width of the church. Raimundinho felt sure it was a sign that the door for the gospel was opening wide.

The first night, everything went well. The second night, several people made professions of faith. But the third night a small riot erupted. The president of the village arrived with a large group and surrounded the house where Raimundinho was preaching. Instead of prayers, stones and curses were hurled at the worshipers inside. The next day, Raimundinho departed for a nearby village. While he was there, a letter arrived from the president of Santa Rosa. The message was clear: "Come back and we'll kill you. We don't want to hear your preaching."

But Raimundinho couldn't forget what he had seen in the clouds. He was determined to return to Santa Rosa, no matter the consequences. As he crossed the river near the village, one of his companions called his attention to a strange shape in the sky. The clouds had gathered into the shape of an enormous black mountain. At the foot of the mountain, was what appeared to be a beast, a jaguar with several heads. To the right of the black mountain was a brilliant white cloud in the form of a horse and rider. As the white cloud approached the black cloud, the shape of the beast dissolved. Once again, Raimundinho believed that a sign had been given.

That night, almost the entire village turned out to hear what the preacher had to say. Surprisingly, the evening passed without a trace of violence. Soon a small church began to take shape in Santa Rosa. Shortly after the initial meetings, a medical missionary team arrived from the United States. In the course of their visit, the team treated 1,097 people, extracted 747 teeth, supplied 505 pairs of eyeglasses, and filled 2,836 prescriptions. Overwhelmed by the love of these strangers, the leaders of the village came to Raimundinho one by one to ask forgiveness for the way they had treated him. They even wanted to know how they might help him continue the work.

Had this man really seen a church in the sky, a many-headed jaguar, a horse and a rider? Or was his overactive imagination simply drawing fantasies in the clouds? Who can say for sure? Whatever the case, one thing is clear: a door that seemed locked and bolted from the inside was opened wide to the love of God—a love that showed itself to the Arapiun Indians, not as a figure in the clouds, but in the shape of ordinary men and women who know that the gospel is more than mere words. It is a way of life.

Is it any wonder that the Creator of everything would sometimes use the heavens to proclaim his glory?

Lord, I am amazed at the way you reveal yourself. But the real wonder is not so much that you place a sign in the sky, but that you stoop down and touch my heart, so that even I can be a sign of your love.

A Vision of a Sealed Jar

I will give them one heart, and put a new spirit within them; I will remove the heart of stone from their flesh and give them a heart of flesh.
(EZEKIEL 11:19)

June Clancy had just settled into her favorite chair, tucking her feet beneath her. The afternoon sun warmed the living room and added to her sense of peace. "Finally," she thought, "a moment's peace." Then she saw it.

"It was just a fleeting image, like a frame of a slide show passing by. I saw a glass jar . . . only the top half. Its lid appeared to be sealed. In the next frame I saw the jar again, but this time a screwdriver was wedged under the lid's edge, breaking the seal.

"I'm not sure how I knew, but I was certain I was that jar with the tightly sealed lid. Somehow, I also realized that the screwdriver represented God's Spirit at work to break open an otherwise unbreakable seal.

"As I prayed, I began to believe that the Lord was going to set me free from the emotional bondage I had suffered since I was a teenager. As far back as I could remember, I had been painfully shy. When I was sixteen, I began dating an older boy who my parents disapproved of. The more they disapproved, the more determined I became to keep dating him, even though it was tearing my family apart. In my stubbornness, I reached a point of decision. I promised myself: 'I'm not going to let them hurt me anymore.' Little did I know I was locking myself into an emotional prison that I would never escape on my own.

"Shortly afterward, I moved with my family to Florida, where I dove headlong into the drug culture of the late sixties: pot, speed, psychedelics. It wasn't mere peer pressure that drove me. Instead, I deliberately started hanging out with kids who lived on the edge. The next thirteen years were a drug-induced haze. The best years of my life weren't stolen from me. I simply threw them away. My motto during those years was a simple one. It went like this: 'No matter what you do or who your are, you can't hurt me!' But the more I protected myself, the more afraid I became. My emotions seemed so powerful—so impossibly hard to control. Finally, when I was twenty-nine, I began to suffer from panic disorder—random, overwhelming anxiety attacks. That's when I finally cried out to Jesus and begged him to help me. I felt utterly broken, nothing but a heap of rubble. But God heard my cry, and four weeks later the anxiety attacks disappeared. They have never returned.

"Still, I had difficulty expressing my emotions. For twenty-four years, I couldn't shed a tear, though I felt like weeping so many times. Eleven years after my conversion, I had the vision of the sealed jar. That's when the Lord began to restore my tears. They came slowly at first but then freely. It was a though a faucet had been turned on at last.

"One Sunday my pastor encouraged those who wanted prayer to stay after the service. My seven-year-old, John Edward, said he wanted to stay, so we both went forward. I stood behind my son, praying silently. When the pastor reached me, his first words were: 'Let her know, Father, she doesn't have to keep it together anymore. She doesn't have to be in control.' I began to shake until my whole body was trembling, and I was weeping with a freedom I had not known. I sobbed and cried out, unafraid of what others around me might think. Then gradually the tears subsided and I felt a tremendous peace.

"I knew then that the lid was finally off. God was removing everything that was trapped inside that jar and fashioning a brand new heart within me. I don't know why he didn't heal me completely when he took away the panic disorder. But I do know that he is healing the sins of my youth and filling me with a deeper freedom and a greater joy."

Create in me a clean heart, O God, and put a new and right spirit within me. Do not cast me away from your presence, and do not take your holy spirit from me. Restore to me the joy of your salvation, and sustain in me a willing spirit.

A Vision of Heaven

He carried me away in the Spirit to a mountain great and high, and showed me the Holy City, Jerusalem, coming down out of heaven from God. It shone with the glory of God, and its brilliance was like that of a very precious jewel, like a jasper, clear as crystal. (REVELATION 21:10)

*S*everal years ago, Gwen Ellis nearly died giving birth to identical twin girls, who survived only a few hours. "I had carried them for only six months," she explained. "They were just too tiny to live. I remember their births vividly. As soon as the first twin was born, the delivery team rushed out of the room with her. The second twin was lodged under my rib cage and the doctor had difficulty delivering her. I was in tremendous pain and the last thing I remember was the doctor saying, 'Give her something for the pain.'

"The next thing I knew, a nurse was shaking me awake. I'm not entirely sure what happened to me on the delivery table, but I'm fairly certain I went into shock while the doctors were busy with the twins. Suddenly I found myself walking on a great green meadow framed by the bluest sky I had ever seen. Later, I could only say it reminded me a little bit of Crater Lake, Oregon. Everything was so sharp and crisp, even the grass had a quality of brittleness to it. I felt absolutely at peace. Suddenly, I heard a voice that said, 'Go back. Ed and Wendy need you.' I thought of my husband and three-year-old daughter and knew that I had a choice to make. Instantaneously, I felt as though I were being pulled backwards toward the earth through a long, dark tube. And then I woke up on the delivery table. When they finally wheeled me out, I was freezing and shaking all over.

"It was so hard to lose those babies, but I knew I still had something to live for. I didn't tell anyone about my experience for a long, long time. It was too precious to have it explained away.

"Afterward I felt so weak. But God was very present. He seemed to be standing behind me holding me up, like when you put your arms under someone whose legs have turned to jelly. His presence was so palpable that I almost felt like we were one. The truth is, we were so close that it would have seemed like a distraction to pray. Eventually, the feeling faded, and I had to work through a lot of grief and anger at losing my daughters. You never really get over it. The hardest time was when my daughter, Wendy, left home to live in Belgium for a year. How my heart ached for those twins! I would have loved having two more girls in my life at that time.

"So many years have passed since that day in the delivery room. It's amazing how one day can contain so much joy and sorrow. But I always felt as though God gave me that experience to comfort me and give me a glimpse of the beautiful place he would provide for my girls—a place where I will one day hold them in my arms and tell them how much I've missed them."

Father, I am glad that you occasionally allow one of us to see past the stars into heaven itself. It comforts me to know that you have prepared a place for those who love you. When I am most discouraged, most lonely for those I have loved and lost, renew my longing for heaven and make hope grow strong in my soul.

A Vision in the Fire

❦

The angel of the Lord appeared to him [Moses] in flames of fire from within a bush. Moses saw that though the bush was on fire it did not burn up. (EXODUS 3:2)

hat's so unusual about a bush on fire? Moses must have seen plenty of fires in the desert, especially in the hottest and driest months of the year. But this was different. An ordinary bush had become the kindling of God. It burned but did not burn up. The flames ran along the branches, but the branches were still strong and green. Suddenly, a voice called out and a divine conversation ensued.

They spoke of many things, God and the man, Moses. God told of his concern for his people's suffering and his plan to deliver Israel from their long years of bondage in Egypt. He showed Moses how to perform miracles, changing his staff into a snake and water into blood. These were signs of power that would eventually terrify Pharaoh and all of Egypt. God told Moses about the key role he would play in Israel's deliverance.

But Moses objected. Who would believe him? He was a fugitive from Egypt. How could he contend with one of the greatest nations on earth? Choose someone else, he told God. Not me. But God was stubborn. And the reluctant Moses became the deliverer of his people.

But why a fiery bush? Why not a brilliant light or a magnificent chariot wheeling across the desert sky? Did God have something in mind when he appeared as fire engulfing an ordinary desert bush? Perhaps it was a sign to the reluctant leader—a sign that would comfort him in the years ahead. Through all the fiery trials that awaited them, Moses and the people of Israel would be preserved because God would dwell in their midst. He would deliver them from every kind of danger and lead the way into a land of freedom

Throughout history, God has blended the natural with the supernatural, what is great with what is not. By forging his strength with our weakness, he formed an alloy so strong that death could not destroy it. This was precisely his plan in the Incarnation, when Jesus became both man and God. This joining of what is divine with what is human is what happens still in our souls. Instead of a destroying fire, the fire of his presence purifies us, leads us out of bondage, and preserves our souls for eternity. Because of God's Spirit, the bush that burned in the desert thousands of years ago still burns in our midst today.

Jesus, I am like that desert bush—completely ordinary until your Spirit lives in me. Make me your kindling, and set my soul on fire. Purify me from every form of evil, no matter how petty or banal. Be the light that leads me into freedom and that helps me to prevail over my distrust and fear and greed. Grant that I may be not a smoking bush or a half-hearted follower of yours but one who burns brightly with the light of your presence.

Epilogue: The Greatest Miracle of All

So Joseph also went up from the town of Nazareth in Galilee to Judea, to Bethlehem the town of David, because he belonged to the house and line of David. He went there to register with Mary, who was pledged to be married to him and was expecting a child. While they were there, the time came for the baby to be born, and she gave birth to her firstborn, a son. She wrapped him in cloths and placed him in a manger, because there was no room for them in the inn. (LUKE 2:4–7)

A teenage girl and a young man left their town in Galilee to travel south to Bethlehem, just outside Jerusalem. The trip couldn't have been easy, especially for the young woman whose womb was stretched to bursting with a pregnancy in its ninth month. We know the story well—too well perhaps to be astonished by the scandal of it all.

Certainly it was scandalous that Mary had conceived a child out of wedlock. We know that. But just like the Jews of her day, we miss the deeper scandal of divine proportions that was developing in her womb. For God had done the unthinkable—he had fathered a child with a human being. And his child would be born as any other human being—covered in blood, screaming for air, and still attached to his mother by a fleshy cord. Together, God and a young woman had produced a child unique in the history of heaven and earth.

But the scandal didn't end with Jesus' birth. For the God who created the earth, who flooded it with judgment in the time of Noah, who destroyed Pharaoh's army by suffocating horse and rider in the waters of the Red Sea, who enabled the Israelites to chase their enemies from the land of promise—this same all-powerful God allowed Mary and Joseph to take custody of his only Son. Arms that God himself had made would cradle Divinity. The plan and purpose of God would be accomplished through weakness, through human limitation, through dependency—through an infant who was as vulnerable to disaster as any human being who ever lived.

This, indeed, is scandal. It overthrows everything we ever thought about God. No longer is he a God who looks down on us from a lofty height, disapproving us, measuring us, and finding us wanting in every way. Instead, he is a tender Father, who cannot bear to be separated from his creatures, who is driven to reveal his true nature by performing the greatest miracle of all—allowing his Son to become one of us, to take us by the hand and lead us out of darkness, to know God even as we are known by him. This is the scandal, this is the miracle, this is the truth that sets us free.

Father, unless you touch my eyes and open them to wonder, I will not be able to perceive what you have done and are doing in the world. Your strategies and plans always take me by surprise. There is so much about you that I cannot comprehend. But what I do know of you causes me to bow before you—before your humility, your kindness, your forgiveness, your holiness, your perfection, your generosity, your courage, your beauty, and your passionate love for me.

ℬIBLIOGRAPHY ๛

Brown, Colin. *Miracles and the Critical Mind* (Grand Rapids, Mich.: William B. Eerdmans, 1984).

Lockyer, Herbert. *All the Miracles of the Bible*. Grand Rapids, Mich.: Zondervan, 1961.

Marshall, Catherine. *Meeting God at Every Turn*. Grand Rapids, Mich.: Chosen, 1980.

McInerny, Ralph. *Miracles: A Catholic View*. Huntington, Ind.: Our Sunday Visitor, 1986.

McKenna, Briege, and Libersat, Henry. *Miracles Do Happen*. Ann Arbor, Mich.: Servant, 1987.

Monden, Louis. *Signs and Wonders*. New York: Desclee, 1966.

Valentine, Mary Hester. *Miracles*. Chicago: Thomas More, 1988.

Wakefield, Dan. *Expect a Miracle*. San Francisco: HarperSanFrancisco, 1995.